Bill

P9-DNK-858

JOURNEYS IN FAITH

Creative Dislocation—The Movement of Grace
Robert McAfee Brown
Speech, Silence, Action! The Cycle of Faith
Virginia Ramey Mollenkott
Hope Is an Open Door
Mary Luke Tobin

By Way of Response

Martin E. Marty

Journeys in Faith
Robert A. Raines, Editor

ABINGDON
Nashville

BY WAY OF RESPONSE

Copyright © 1981 by Abingdon

All rights reserved.
No part of this book may be reproduced in any manner
whatsoever without written permission of the publisher
except brief quotations embodied in critical articles
or reviews. For information address Abingdon,
Nashville, Tennessee.

Library of Congress Cataloging in Publication Data

MARTY, MARTIN E. 1928-
  By way of response.
  (Journeys in faith)
  1. Marty, Martin E., 1928-   2. Lutheran Church—Clergy—Bi-
ography. 3. Clergy—United States—Biography. 4. Christian union. 5.
Church and the world. I. Title. II. Series.
BX8080.M27A32   284.1'3 [B]   80-20042

ISBN 0-687-04477-4

Scripture quotations unless otherwise noted are from the Revised Standard
Version of the Bible, copyrighted 1946, 1952, © 1971, 1973 by the Division of
Christian Education of the National Council of the Churches of Christ in the
U.S.A. and used by permission.

MANUFACTURED BY THE PARTHENON PRESS AT
NASHVILLE, TENNESSEE, UNITED STATES OF AMERICA

To Joseph Sittler
a gracefully natural mentor

Contents

Editor's Foreword

People inside and outside the church today are engaged in a profound revisioning of the faith journey. Wanting to honor our own heritage and to be nourished by our roots, we also want to discern the signs of the kingdom now, and to move into the 1980s with a lean, biblical, ecumenical, and human faith perspective.

The Journeys in Faith series is offered to facilitate this revisioning of faith. Reflecting on the social justice openings of the 1960s and the inward searching of the 1970s, these books articulate a fresh integration of the faith journey for the years ahead. They are personal and social. Authors have been invited to share what has been happening to them in their faith and life in recent years, and then to focus on issues that have become primary for them in this time.

We believe that these lucidly written books will be widely used by study groups in congregations, seminaries, colleges, renewal centers, orders, and denominations, as well as for personal study and reflection.

Our distinguished authors embody a diversity of experience and perspective, which will provide many points of identification and enrichment for readers. As we enter into the pilgrimages shared in these books we will find resonance, encouragement, and insight for a fresh appropriation of our faith, toward personal and social transformation.

Martin E. Marty's contribution to this series is unique in its retrospective glimpse of what's been happening in the world and church over the last forty years. A precocious as well as professional historian, Marty recalls the power and glory of his childhood apprehension of the faith, growing up Lutheran in a small midwestern town. He gives us distinct and colorful snapshots of college and seminary days, the years of parish ministry, the ecumenical openings of *The Christian Century,* and the academic context of The University of Chicago. Marty, the mapmaker, learned as he went, always observing. He was nourished by the strength of deep and narrow roots, transcending provincialism with abiding continuities. Erasmus and Luther are well integrated in this man and this book. Marty's "life project" came to be a matter of conceiving how dedicated groups should relate to one another, how the one and the many might live together in civility but with commitment. He describes how he turned from a "God of prey," requiring mission as proselytism, to a "God of promise," inviting mission as responsiveness. He asks, what happens when narrow, particularistic certainties fade; how is faith heroic in an age of Christian humanism? A tribal man himself, honoring his heritage, he is a pluralistic man as well, respecting and appreciating the traditions of others. There is a sanity and measured hopefulness in these pages, affirming as they do the life and work of the local congregation.

Marty, the storyteller, tells his own story of no major breaches of continuity, crises, or rebellions with well-tempered irenic wit. He takes his readers with him from childhood to middle age in such a way that we retrace our own journeys with widened eyes and a fresh responsiveness. Quite a gift.

Robert A. Raines

We do not exist because we think. Man is the son of God and not brought into being by thinking. We are called into society by a mighty entreaty, "Who art thou, man, that I should care for thee?" And long before our intelligence can help us, the new-born individual survives this tremendous question by his naive faith in the love of his elders. We grow into society on faith, listening to all kinds of human imperatives. Later we stammer and stutter, nations and individuals alike, in the effort to justify our existence by responding to this call. We . . . wish to follow the deepest questions, the central call which goes straight to the heart, and promises our soul the lasting certainty of being inscribed in the book of life.

—Eugen Rosenstock-Huessy,
I Am an Impure Thinker

1
Invitatory*

In the long ago, steeples dominated the American landscape. Until the skyscrapers rose, church domes made the boldest silhouettes on the horizons of cities. Nowhere did temple towers stand out more clearly than against the backdrop of small town roofs.

Twenty-five years after he left one such village, a father brought his sons back to marvel at the splendor of a St. Paul's church in a town on the plains. As the touring family entered the community, they came to a new St. Paul's along the highway. It was a forthright building whose stained glass, on examination, turned out to be worth a visit. But the father soon grew restless. Compared to its

*In churches with more formal worship, this term refers to a psalm or phrase sung in early morning services as a call for prayerful response. The words assigned to the congregation are called the "responsory."

grand predecessor, he thought, the new building must be like a small chicken coop in the shadow of a great barn on any of the nearby farms.

Oh, the old church up the hill! The pioneer builders thought of it as the cathedral of the plains. Their heirs cut its image to size. It became merely a cathedral, after people in adjacent towns vied to reach nearer the sky with ever higher roofs. St. Paul's finally compensated, regaining its primacy when it came to boast a major pipe organ, the gift of an eccentric donor on the eve of the Great Depression. The man's own father had been the organist and the man remembered spending many Sabbaths in range of the elemental roar of that instrument. The pew in which the child sat vibrated, and the sound waves caused tremors in the floor that his short legs never reached.

In years to come as the boy grew to manhood he wandered from this sanctuary, but its scale never left his imagination. He found himself emotionally ready for his first gape at the length and height of Amiens and Ulm cathedrals. The windows at Chartres were as stunning as the guidebooks promised, but it was St. Paul's that prepared him for the way the breaking sun hinted at worlds beyond the stained glass. The arches of his boyhood church aspired to the very heavens. Above the point at which they finally gave out and met above the chancel, a mural of the ascending Christ added to the illusion of endless upward soaring. The father remembered being in that chancel on Christmas Eve. There he gasped out his programmed lines to a congregation whose more remote participants stretched into distant recesses. That crowd made it easy for him to cope with the sight of huge audiences on later days at St. Peter's in Rome.

O come, let us sing unto the Lord; . . .
Let us come before his presence with thanksgiving, . . .
For the Lord is a great God, and a great King above all gods. . . .
O come, let us worship and bow down. (Ps. 95:1-6 KJV)

That invitatory still sounded in his mind after so many years. It was natural to respond by kneeling before the great God, the great King, whose house this was. The word that thundered weekly through the gloom from St. Paul's pulpit arrived with a scope to match the architecture. No mundane moralisms or prattled book reviews ever passed from the preacher's lips to waste the time of congregations. Most messages were designed to jolt the pieties of harmless burghers and drouth-stricken farmers. They always returned even though the constant prayers for rain brought no response from the heavens.

The jealous God of Israel was the deity who made his presence felt. His scoldings held the group together and threatened potentially wayward lives. Decades later, to at least one of the hearers, now an adult, neither the humdrum violence shown on television nor the retold horrors of European genocide seemed utterly foreign experiences to the father. As a child he had often heard sermons about the ancient day when the sun stood still at Gibeon, until Israel "took vengeance on their enemies." Never could he forget the reason behind the subsequent massacre, as Joshua unfolded it: "Every man they smote with the edge of the sword, until they had destroyed them, and they did not leave any that breathed" (Josh. 11:14). "For it was of the Lord to harden their hearts, that they should come against Israel in battle, that he might destroy them utterly, and that they might have no favour, but that he might destroy them, as the Lord commanded Moses" (Josh. 11:20 KJV).

No hard-hearted Amorites or other foreign tribes served to push the people of God together on the local plains, so the members of St. Paul's were taught to seek milder vengeance in the name of the Lord of Hosts by snubbing the members of another church two blocks away. Theirs was a congregation of God whose only manifest vice was that they belonged to a variant of the same communion. Their ancestors, it seems, came from Europe on a different set of boats and established themselves independently.

Such long-distance enemies, however, came to be ignored too easily, so the preacher had to look closer to home in order to locate offenders against the jealous Judge of Israel. Thus one week— could the details really have been as grim as the boys' father recalled them?—the minister "denied Christian burial on holy ground" to some young parishioners. On a lark, evidently impelled by hardened hearts, they had spent an evening at a roadhouse. An onrushing train demolished their automobile and ended their earthly lives on their midnight ride home. Dancing, especially dancing at a public house where they might meet and be tempted to marry local Canaanites, was mocking the God of Israel. But the plains parsons were selective about moral issues. Theirs was the wettest church body in Christendom. All through Prohibition the ministers always knew where to get a case of illegal home brew for which to compete during softball breaks at pastoral conferences.

As for those abandoned dancers, they were supposed to become object lessons in immorality and eternal punishment. But life in the town went on the next week as before, a sign to the child that no one really believed that those unrepentant unfortunates were suffering on the spit in eternal flames. Townspeople still were friendly, though hard times gave them little to smile about. They continued to love their offspring, and these children knew it. The steeple of St. Paul's beckoned as before to a heeding firmament, the bells rang out cordially, and citizens greeted their pastor as the amiable neighbor and friend he truly was whenever he closed his black book and hung up his gown.

To balance his fearsome dispensings of divine justice, the same man often spoke benignly of the other face of God. To be sure, parents and the church school did their part by supplying words of tenderness and gestures of warmth in a climate of sheltering nurture. But also on other Sundays from the pulpit came frequently graceful words on a text the preacher declared to be his favorite, 1 Timothy 1:15-16: "Christ Jesus came into the world to save sinners; of whom I am chief. Howbeit for this cause I obtained mercy, that in me first Jesus Christ might shew forth all long-suffering, for a pattern to them which should hereafter believe on him to life everlasting" (KJV).

Each time he told the congregants to substitute their own name for the "I" in the scripture. The outline of the sermon was always the same; only his accompanying anecdotes varied. The father of the boys remembered that these came packaged in King James English in the sources from which the minister cribbed them, collections of antique pulpit discourses. And to match the threats and scoldings of his spoken word on any day they sang chorales like the Christmas hymn whose word about an enfleshed God often helped the now-grown boy stand tall:

> . . . Tell abroad His goodness proudly
> Who our race hath honored thus
> *That He deigns to dwell with us* . . .
> Christian Keimann, translated by Catherine Winkworth

Reminiscence of such scenes and sounds that had never really left him filled the back of his mind while the father was explaining the new church windows to his eager-to-leave family. Abruptly the current pastor discovered the tourists and asked if they had any questions.

"I do like the new church," said the father, "but I am more

eager to show the family the church in which I was christened, the grand old St. Paul's."

"Well," said the minister, "it's a good thing then that you came along just now. This autumn they're going to level it."

"How could they do that to such a magnificent building?"

Came the reply: "Oh, what use is it? After the congregation outgrew it, they converted it to a recreation hall. But that didn't really work out too well for sports like volleyball and basketball. You see, the walls were too confining and the ceiling was too low."

More than half the people I know, urban or rural, black or white, Jew or Gentile, could stand in imagination with me, the father in that story, at a place which represented their invitation to what I am going to call their tribe. We at St. Paul's were tribal, which was good, because we thus knew who we were and whom to trust. We were also tribal*ist*, which was bad, because we did not really know who others were and were taught to mistrust them.

In *Idols of the Tribe* Harold Isaacs tells how the Kikuyus in Kenya stand before their elders at the moment of their rites of passage to swear to the deity they named the sacred mother of their tribe, "I will never leave the House of Muumbi." At St. Paul's our weekly invitatory came as a demand never to leave our tribal house. Modern elders who care for their young, find some way figuratively to huddle with them within walls that one day will come to look confining and under ceilings that may turn out to be too low. Many adolescents strain against the confinement of their pledges and look for breathing spaces beyond those. Embarrassment about childhood formation is standard fare in tales about Oedipal rejection, personal identity crises, and the search for new outlooks in life.

Not all children remember such invitations or demands. In their case no tribe imposed its rites. Those who rage against their own version of a House of Muumbi sometimes foolishly envy those who never knew such symbolic shelter. At a Roman Catholic university, not long after the Second Vatican Council, some students cheered a blasphemously furious ex-priest who was scorning Mother Church. I asked them why the applause. "You'll never understand," said one, "what an identity crisis the Catholic Church gave each one of us." I wondered aloud if they knew how lucky they were ever to have belonged to anything that was potent enough to give them an identity over which to have a crisis.

Wanderers from the Great Plains were not the only ones who carried traces of tribes wherever they went. Manhattan pedestrians look cosmopolitan. Some of them have grown up so mobile that they never experienced rootage. But most of them emerged from a ghetto or a shtetl something like the congregation on the plains. In urban wards or rural valleys other moderns heard invitations or experienced molding pressures of the sort we felt in our chapels. As for the rebels against the past among them, were theirs only acts of bolder imagination or more creative rage than ours? Were we dullards to keep some ties to ancestral piety and outlook, never to join them in spitting words of disdain against clan origins in the name of liberation?

The legacy of most tribes is mixed. The elders who transmitted severe codes and then tempered them with warm words spent no time preparing us to respond to people and spirits of other groups. Some persons spend their lives in isolation with their tribe. They need never test their traditions. Others become aware of outsiders, only then to retreat into the absolutism of their old ways. They have to busy themselves endlessly reinforcing their insecure egos and redrawing threatened boundaries around their life-spaces. Committed but uncivil, they are not necessarily more dangerous than the superficially civil but uncommitted. Some of them become window-shoppers in the marketplace of values, never-satisfied spiritual shoplifters who evoke a sense of pathos among their more passionate contemporaries. Such soulless generations help create the void that tyrannies fill, and can become converts to their totalisms.

In the small town, a sense of shelter and distance temporarily kept from view the aggression that fills most pages of history and the images in the mass media of communication. Violence between persons and groups is the dirty but open secret of history. Religious history has only made it more ugly. As the third millennium after Christ approaches in a crowded world with plentiful weapons and ideologies, it is easy to picture how the good of the tribal way will be lost amid the perils of tribalism. In our time, speech turns to soliloquy and the ideas of competing groups are perverted into solipsisms.

This was to have been an epoch of international and interfaith understanding, if not convergence. Instead, groups huddle convulsively and then break out against others. Conflict occurs on all scales, from those between huge blocks of nations to minuscule gatherings of fanatics. Lest conflict between them stand a chance of being creative, tribalists frequently attach religious symbols to their claims and their potential disappears. Those who see their jealous gods hardening the hearts of others lose all responsiveness to them and aggression becomes most vicious.

To take our rather harmless example: at the church on the plains and the others of its communion, the elders insisted that theirs was "*the* true visible church on earth." Beyond it, God might take care of occasional stranded Robinson Crusoes on churchly island outposts, far from our exclusive body. Such an outlook prevented the members from praying with Christians from other houses, whether in the company of military chaplains before battle, amidst the civic pieties of baccalaureate services and the Boy Scouts, or even at table grace. Not all the other tribes were so fierce on this point, but the chronicles contain accounts of many only slightly less demarcated ones. Late in this century, the experts now tell us, those sects that most arrogantly billboard their unique hold on truth and are most vicious toward others will prosper at the expense of the more open-minded groups. This fact tells much about the gods of twentieth-century tribalists and searchers.

As for the genteel but uncommitted, their gods seem too passive to be jealous and too neutral to save. These contemporaries cherish a church called "Old Trinity" to remind them of divinity, but its ringing bells echo against uncaring heavens. If once such half-believers owned roots, now only dried-out cut flowers linger. These persons never hear an invitatory that calls for response, and hardly notice the absence of deep convictions within themselves.

The road for the journey of life does not pass between only the camps of the convinced but uncivil and of the civil but uncommitted. If it did, others on the journey could simply protect themselves against the first and build empathy for or try to stir the second. To settle for such classifying would satisfy those who say that on any issue the world can always be divided in two groups—or the one who says that the world is divided in two kinds of people: those who divide the world in two kinds of people and those who do not. Instead, numerous fellow travelers, who merit our observation, are as passionate as the tribalists, yet they are somehow responsive to those who do not share their own outlook. Their counterparts on the same journey are people who, instinctively responsive, find ways to be fervent about their philosophies or creeds.

Both of these latter companies are so small and their thinking is so rarely outlined that the public has difficulty locating them. Therefore, old stereotypes survive to serve as the last words in human understanding. According to this conventional wisdom, strong groups are strong precisely because their members persist in being blind to the values of others. Following the same unimaginative law of history, weak wills are supposed to be capable only of generating bland tolerance. They can never combine into groups of the convinced. Responsiveness, which ought to be the accompaniment of mature faith, in current culture turns out to be the symptom of wan half-faith. According to the critics, only crusading and inquisitorial religion is *real* religion.

Can we now begin to reconceive the way of response in order to be ready for a new epoch? Is it possible to work toward the development of cultures in which strong groups can turn civil by convincement, while people of civil outlook can hold to convictions of the sort that profound believers always have claimed? I cannot trace steps to the beginning of a journey that committed me to addressing such questions. Few companions along the way recall clearly a day in adolescence when they defined their life project. Only a few hear voices or open books that address them directly. Enlightenment about vocation comes rarely with the flash of an "aha!" or a conversion that arrives with the suddenness of rebirth. We choose a turn in the path in answer to one hint and, after trial and errors, find a way back to another.

The idea of spending the energies of a life conceiving how dedicated groups should relate to one another was not prime on my early agenda. Most other tribes were at best remote abstractions. The economy of drouth and the Depression allowed for no travel. Each of our sons had journeyed farther from home by their twelfth week than their parents had by their twelfth year. The media were not yet then so pervasive as now. They could not make other ways seem immediately accessible to the isolated young. Old copies of *National Geographic* in the classroom and a tiny, but virtually read-through, town library were, in such cases, the only windows on a world beyond the local.

The only nearby people who had a rightful claim on the word I am here seizing and translating for other purposes—the tribe—were Winnebagos on a reservation ten miles away. As one who aspired then to be a poet and as a fervent provincial, I devoured the writings of poet John G. Neihardt. The house in which he did his early writings stood but one town to the north on reservation soil. His *Black Elk Speaks* opened the world of the First Americans for me, but no one in our ken seemed to notice the local Indians themselves, either as enemies or problems or friends. Did they exist?

As for the heirs of those ancients from whom we drew childhood concepts of tribes, the Jews, not one lived within sixty miles. Experts on Jewish-Christian relations sometimes claim that we who were orthodox were always taught that they were "Christ-killers." I remember no such teaching, at least not any that focused on Jews more than on the Romans or the American "chief of sinners" who occupied our pulpit and pews. To us, blacks were colored people who bused through from Piney Woods, but whose inspiring choirs symbolized no threat and little promise. Four centuries after the Protestant Reformation we did still fight mental battles against the Pope and Turk. The Turk of our day was a hemisphere away. The people of the Pope, who we *were* taught was the very Antichrist, never did anything worse than storm down the hill from Guardian Angels School to defeat the basketball teams of "the true visible church on earth." Returning missionaries enchanted us with stories of the boring and probably idolatrous hours Orientals spent at prayer wheels. They taught us not to exterminate such remote spinners of wheels. Theirs may not have been sophisticated exercises in comparative religion, but Asian faith did not become the negative reinforcer of our group. Only the threatening deviants among us or the beguilers from that near-match church down the street could serve to look like enemies of the Lord of Hosts and the elect people.

The critics of dwellers in "the Big Sky" country say that we lived with illusions. The limitless plains and sand hills, with their sparse and friendly populations, bred an expansive spirit. Citizens there dreamed that they could always escape to a farther frontier if a threatening group encroached. They did not need to draw their wagons into a circle. They simply moved on, whether actually or spiritually. Feeling cooped up or alienated, in this account of things, had to be a trauma only of New York Jews or ethnic Catholics crowded into Great-Lakes-area metropolises. Looking back, I wonder, Did I need some illusions in order to set out on my course? Realism would temper expectations later, along with a way of life that is almost overwhelmed by urban pluralism. Maybe the atypicality of existence on the plains bought me time and space for generating wonder in the midst of a disenchanted world. Whatever the occasions, such beginnings produced a momentum that, given what I now know about the problems of human interaction, could otherwise have disappeared early in the journey.

Even in that protected world people had some reasons to be on guard toward outsiders or resentful about them. While we were part-Swiss strays from across the river into the community, one side of our family and most sides of the parish were of German background. Even though the members were all unquestioning patriots, only fifteen years earlier they had suffered because of their ethnic ties to the rapacious Hun, the atrocious Boche, the enemy in World War I. And now they looked for villains to explain their setbacks. As victims of the drouth that turned the sand hills to the Dust Bowl, they cast around until they fingered

Bolsheviks and Democrats. But these were mildly chronic, not acute occasions for their sticking together.

The chronicles of life journeys include remembrances of roads not taken, projects each of us rejected. Why, for example, did I not convert childhood puzzles and wonderments into a basic theological inquiry? Some bearded giants who were baptized in our same communion, Ludwig Feuerbach and Karl Marx and Friedrich Nietzsche, had posed a challenge a century before. They asked, Behind all the tribes, is there a God at all? Is the sacred name useful? Does it mean anything? Was the jealous God of Israel and the rescuer of the chief of sinners a mere human projection, an illusion without a future? Did the symbol of this divine fantasy retard the development of Superman or Superforce? Bearded respondents of our own broader traditions, the giants of the German theological heritage, were later available as models to our new generation.

That set of issues never became obsessive. No child would use his language but a phrase of Martin Buber covers the reason for rejecting one choice quite well: for me, God was "addressed," not "expressed." God was "Thou" for personal engagement more than "It" for objective examination. It is hard for children with such an attitude to recall a time when they did not recognize that God was not something to be rolled out on stage in order to satisfy the proof seekers. Nor did we ever hear from the pulpit or anywhere else the promise of any satisfying answer to the problem of evil. Why were hearts hardened, Canaanite towns destroyed, some sinners unsaved? As son of the church organist, I had attended many funerals. I saw the tears but heard no philosophical explanation of their occasions, and concluded that the best one could hope for was to live in the face of evil and its conditions. This, it was often pointed out, the Crucified One himself had done.

Those who do not feel called to devote a life to such subjects of mystery have worlds of other projects open to them. More interesting to me have been questions in the context of human history. In a world whose people act as if unseen powers are bearing down on their universes in such a way that they must make response, what do we do about the responses, and how do we regard the people who make them? Jacob Burckhardt used masculine terms that need translation: "The one point accessible to us, the one eternal center of all things" is "man, suffering, striving, doing, as he is and was and ever shall be." Invitatory words through the years pulled me to the field of storytelling, at first in one community of faith and then as a historian amid interactive communities. My response describes a terrain but not the path. A path only gradually emerged in the company of colleagues who follow its directions despite frequent distractions and occasional meanderings. Among them, I began to isolate an issue and perhaps some images for the journey.

Let me lead into them by comparing a person's life to what a favorite philospher of mine, Eugen Rosenstock-Huessy, once wrote about a volume. "One book is about one thing; at least the good ones are." The most rich and varied lives I contend, are also "about" one thing. Not Rosenstock-Huessy's at first glance: "I am an impure thinker, I am hurt, swayed, shaken, elated, disillusioned, shocked, comforted, and I have to transmit my mental experiences lest I die. And although I may die." An impure thinker he was, but never an undirected one. His life was finally about his motto, *respondeo etsi mutabor,* "I respond although I shall be changed." Responding did not mean being an antenna constantly turning for a signal. His life was not like a sponge or blotter that only soaks up substance from others, a mirror to bounce back images. A forceful ego was there, as assuredly as in José Ortega y Gasset's self-summary, "I am I and my circumstances." This points to a perfect tension between the freedom of self and the fate of environment. *To respond:* this places the respondent in the zone of personalist world views, like those of Emmanuel Mounier and Gabriel Marcel: *esse est co-esse, Sein ist Mit-Sein,* to be is to be with. For the scholarly Rosenstock-Huessy it also meant more than being merely bookish: "The presence of one living soul among the three million volumes of a great library offers sufficient proof against the notion that the secret of their soul is to be found by reading those three million books." With marvelous audacity he worked his primal vision into an outline of the epochs of learning in the West. First came *credo ut intelligam,* I believe in order to understand. Then followed *cogito ergo sum,* I think, therefore I am. And now, for our generations, *respondeo etsi mutabor.* He commented about the three in order: truth is divine and has been divinely revealed; truth is pure and can be scientifically stated; but now, "truth is vital and must be socially represented." That was what, at heart, his life was about.

Martin Buber had a career of great complexity, posed symbolically as it was between East and West at Jerusalem, or between arcane Hasidic lore and patent secular philosophy. Yet his *I and Thou* captured the whole trajectory of his life. So did "reverence for life" for Albert Schweitzer. Paul Tillich roamed philosophically and personally, but *The Courage to Be* reveals his core. Pope John XXIII in his *Journal of a Soul* tried to prune the tendrils of his life to make and keep it simple. His life, like Martin Luther King's contradictory-appearing one, found coherence in the theme of "reconciliation." Whoever takes pains to conjure the image of especially vivid people, be they the school custodian, the track coach, a remembered teacher, or a sage at a nursing home, will find similar coherences in the lives of the less well known.

Many of us build on convictions unwittingly brought from our cozy huddles, and then enlarge or confirm them through literary refinements, with many mentors as guides. As an American religious historian in the face of the most jumbled and competitive melange of religiosities the world has ever known, my project almost naturally came to focus around the philosophical theme of "the one and the many" and the political problem of "pluralism." To trace positive connections between the plural tribes, the concepts of "tolerance" or "civility" were tempting but inadequate. For me no root covers the theme as well as *respondere*. It includes the reply to an invitation or a command; being like a responsory to the invitation of God establishes conviction; being responsive to the call of other people assures their integrity and civil peace; being responsible to the call of principle grounds ethics.

This story of a storyteller is not an autobiography. I have taken pains not to live an externally vivid life, one which could obscure the importance of listening, the impulse to watch, the patience to do research, or the writer's search for the silence which is never silent enough and the night which is never night enough (Kafka). Thus I took pains to be born minutes too late to take part in the Second World War, and have never stood for any kind of election. With luck, I shall leave no name or stamp on legislation, police blotters, scientific discoveries, or cures. It would be nice to weather no breakdowns or divorces or breaches of continuity in life. This career can be full if its possessor never rides a space shuttle or an undersea vehicle. It will not be necessary for me to form a spiritual cult or to have a unique incandescent experience of God.

Yet while tracking the ways of humans who have gone before, or observing their todays, many have been the times when in the library or at the lectern, whether in the night silence or under the television light glare, I have known excitements as a project took form. At such moments, after some delicate rightings, it sometimes turns out that the trajectory looks true. Microscopic hair on the spine abruptly stand out, and adrenalin surges. For a moment the chaos at the edges of life does not threaten the center, and the terror or violence in history recedes. Some would call the mild eurekas at such moments the evidence of a "sense of wonder." But on this journey, such a way of responding comes as close as anything I crave to the sense of the presence of God.

For comparing journeys, the student years, which need little elaboration here, represent some pushing out, but against resistant walls and under a low ceiling at first. In pretheological work, nothing and no one encouraged any outreach. Students in urban settings prepared for religious vocations, but, on principle, there was never to be a trace of exposure, scholastic or existential, to any other tribe than our own. A civilizing public library beckoned five afternoons a week. My taste shifted subtly from poetry to art, from art to art history, from art history to history history, and finally to the religious history that became the subject of a profession. With the turn of many pages, old limits gave way. The exclusivism forced on us in the huddle did not do justice to the glimpses of the *oikoumene*, that larger world which was available only in print while we were denied living contacts with it. A few sympathetic faculty members gave encouragement to our breed and helped head off any impulses we might have had to rebel.

The seminary world proved to be more liberating. Formally, the walls remained confining. A school that warned against the evils of sectarianism in the form of the Jehovah's Witnesses and Latter-day Saints was officially as closed off as the groups named. A faculty host who one day

introduced a guest Jesuit scholar made clear that the priest
would discuss his translation of a grammar and was not to
say anything of a theological nature. Survivors of Nazi
concentration camps and heroic advocates for the Jews
came to us as heroes, but they were never to be seen as
heroes of faith. They were compelled to lecture, never to
preach, because they lacked credentials in our church.
From the devastated universities of Germany some
students began to migrate to our seminary, but half of these
were kin to our tribe. They kept the introverted spirit alive.
We collected funds at the dining hall table to support
German theological students, only to have boxes raided by
these partisans who wanted no food to reach students at
Marburg, where dangerous heretic scholar Rudolf Bult-
mann taught.

Against such forces, some giants in the earth on the faculty
and in the senior student body tutored us for better days.
Because they did so while under restrictions without showing
signs of bitterness, they gave encouragement to us in our
projects. In our communion, people often speak of their
"tower experience," after the model of Martin Luther's
discovery for himself of the Christian gospel in the monastery
tower. He said it occurred *in cloaca,* in the outhouse, as it were.
Many of us had our tower experience as we heard brilliant
expoundings of texts from Paul, and each made some of
them our own. Such courses kept most of us from either
mental sluggishness or late-adolescent religious crisis, as
fashionable as those were in the seminary world. Not to put
too intellectual a point on the struggle, I think that the
substance of these Pauline writings brought such a sense of
liberation that it swept counteremotions aside.

Three passages appear so frequently in my notes and files
from those years—one of them became a text for the homily
at our wedding eucharist and others the text for those
instruments of torture called student sermons—that it is no

wonder that they remain the direction-finders on my map. In my mind, they merited being taken as literally as our more rigid mentors wanted us to interpret their favorite parts of the Bible.

The first of them breaks down confining walls and raises low ceilings: "For all things are yours, whether Paul or Apollos or Cephas or the world or life or death or the present or the future, all are yours; and you are Christ's; and Christ is God's" (I Corinthians 3:21-23). The phrase about Paul or Apollos or Cephas addresses what today we would call the problem of denominationalism. Paul lost his temper as he thought of Corinthian Christian tribalists. They huddled together with the boast that they belonged to Paul *or* Apollos *or* Cephas *or* Christ. For them and their successors in Christian equivalents to Houses of Muumbi, Paul had only one word. It was a question that in their faces seemed to be spit out as a sneer, "Is Christ divided?" That became the only important question behind Christian intertribal relations and determined the character of responses. But Paul also moved beyond the Christian ecumenical aura to the larger sphere in which *panta*, "all things" are yours. The historian in me has always been amazed to see how untraditional Paul was when he left out the past, but he radically included "all things" present and future.

Then came another invitatory that demanded response, II Corinthians 5:17: "Therefore, if any one is in Christ, he is a new creation; the old has passed away, behold, the new has come." The Greek for "he is a new creation," *kainé ktisis*, can also read, "there is a new world." This meaning is compelling in light of the next phrase about the new order having arrived. Computers and German theologians say that the "in Christ" formula and its parallels occur 164 times in the New Testament. They designate a kind of circumstance or envelope in which the believer is found or

identified with Christ. At many tiring turns along the
journey it is a spur to think of human history, marked as it is
by violence and terror, by hatred and self-reinforcement, as
also and already a new order, a new world. It seldom looks
that way.

More audacious is Colossians 1:15-17: "Christ is the
image of the invisible God, the firstborn of all creation, for
in him all things were created, in heaven and earth, visible
and invisible, whether thrones or dominions or principali-
ties or authorities—all things were created through him and
for him. He is before all things, and in him all things hold
together." It is hard to know what this can mean, but "all
things" has to include the curriculum and the library, the
catalog and the phone book, the very worlds that naturally
look incoherent.

Much of my walk today is in the company of secularists,
Jews, or ignorers who do not gain their identity by
reference to such claims as these. But I have always found it
timesaving to show these companions that such assertions
are part of what constitute the Christian outlook. They will
know us best if they begin with such texts. Such an approach
is promising and demanding, because they will certainly be
puzzled as they make a game of looking for evidences that
we really believe it. Second, it shows them something of
what helps formulate our problem: how to respond to them
in the light of such encompassing visions. And, finally, it
challenges them to find out what are the groundworks of
their own lives, what in their belief scandalizes us, what
should be as jarring in our ears as these texts are in theirs.

The first call to response, however, occurs within the
Christian community. Whatever may be the size of any
cathedrals built in the scope of these texts, whether Amiens
or Ulm or Chartres; whatever the style of university or
library believers will establish to house those who ponder it,
they will all demonstrate what the minister said of the

village church. "The walls were too confining and the ceiling was too low."

Old files from classes on sermonizing and souvenirs of wedding homilies addressed to us are only paper, not life. Vivid as these scriptures remain, they were never the only preoccupations of those years. Thus when ecumenical impulses were formally denied, many of us did what we later read Denis de Rougemont confessing: he formed his own one-person ecumenical movement to express instant communion with people who were supposed to be beyond his range. In the world of art and architecture, the Abbé Paul Couturier spoke to our hearts when he told how for religious art he trusted genius apart from the question of faith. Weekly stops at a tuberculosis sanitarium bred pastoral instincts among busloads of us seminarians who were sullen en route and giddy while returning. We had just visited people who, thanks to a barbaric numbering system, lay in beds marked by numerals that indicated how near death each was. Given the right, or wrong, number, we knew our counselee would be gone the next week. "All things are yours. . . ." Whether the illicit ecumenical contacts or the world of Couturier's art or life and death at the sanitarium. . . .

Then, on the eve of ordination, came a surprising turn and a new influence in life. Yes, surprising but not grim, for the way of response is full of caprice and good nature alongside the violence and discipline. Years later I would see this aspect in a type that Hugo Rahner called God's "grave-merry" person. Such a believer has taken the measure of the cramping boundaries of existence and for that reason, or in spite of it, is a person of tears *and* laughter, a person of invincible security and a kind of spiritual elegance. Perhaps no one can fully embody these extremes, but even an imaginary one can provide excellent company for the journey. I am going to speak about a creature who had more impact on my life than any of the mentors mentioned so far: Rosenstock-Huessy and Buber, Mounier and Marcel, Ortega and Burckhardt, Tillich and Pope John, Paul and . . . well, not Paul, then.

One Sunday afternoon, as an act of protest against the closing of the seminary library on weekends before Monday term papers were due, a classmate invented his footnotes for such a paper. The name among them that struck me most was that of "Bibfeldt, Franz." During the next three summers as this inventive friend and I teamed to make a living by icing Burlington railroad cars, I distracted him from the work he found otherwise distasteful by interviewing him about this theologian. Gradually Bibfeldt began to take on consistency and life.

By the final years of seminary we were studding the student magazine with references to our common mentor. His epigraphs appeared as filler, his portrait was scheduled soon to appear. Professor Jaroslav Jan Pelikan, Jr., now of Yale, then of the seminary, solemnly announced that the sequel to his recent book *From Luther to Kierkegaard* was to be *From Kierkegaard to Bibfeldt*. Whereupon Arthur Carl Piepkorn, late author of the mammoth *Profiles in Belief*, with just as solemn a tongue in just as scholarly a cheek, began to take issue with the Pelikan interpretation. The librarian joined the harmless conspiracy by cataloging the corpus of Bibfeldtiana while the bookstore saw to it that Bibfeldt was always "on order" but, as in the library, never available, because of the long waiting lists. As faculty members caught on to the commotion, they added to the lore; so did a couple of publishing houses.

The Bibfeldt invention was never as funny, of course, as we in the thigh-slapping circles that gathered at an adjacent pub liked to think. The history of academic hoaxes is as old and dreary as the academy itself, and the list of invented names in scholarly footnotes threatens to be as long as are authentic ones. But Bibfeldt somehow lived on. He has enjoyed his minutes on the Columbia Broadcasting System, his byline on prime time television, his name in several lectures or articles and in the donor's list at a Chicago White Sox benefit. Misled notables have autographed their pictures for the Bibfeldt Foundation collection, sometimes acknowledging in their greetings the value of his work for them.

The Bibfeldt ideology has changed after twenty-five years; he embodies the principle of responding-although-he-will-be-changed gone awry. His coat of arms displays the ever-changing god Proteus atop a weather vane, and his motto is the Spanish line, "I dance to the tune that is played." But at midcentury Bibfeldt was most useful for our satirical comment on one aspect of our own system, our own way of reinforcing our House of Muumbi. To cite this here is not to suggest that our own system was uniquely obtuse or perverse—Unitarian and Episcopalian pranksters have discovered targets just as obvious. I have no doubt and some suspicion that latter-day Bibfeldts have even been invented to keep his inventors in their place.

It so happened that to reinforce our tribe at the moment when it was emerging in the turbulence of postwar American pluralism, some professors found it more necessary than before to devise props. They then converged on new defenses of the absolute authority of the Bible, literally interpreted on their private premises. The most convenient way to promote full assurance was to minimize the human element in its authorship. God let inspired writers keep their own styles, but they became virtual secretaries to the deity. They were like mechanical subjects of divine dictation, and as such their errant minds were themselves purged from the transmission process. But the mechanical dictation theory was curiously absent from the list of acceptable interpretations, thanks to the survival of older Lutheran, and thus more open, views of biblical authority.

Whenever a professor of the rigid sort would set forth his views on the subject somewhere along "in the seventeenth place," after the preceding sixteen had fit perfectly the template of the mechanical dictation theory, he would assert with sudden and vigorous rhetorical flourishes, "but we do not teach the mechanical dictation theory." That was to take care of that. The colloquialists among the students rudely called Bibfeldtianism a "wwwhhhtt" theology because of the suddenness of its address to problems. This way of getting out of a jam was, in more refined language, the relieving of paradox by sanctified rhetorical excess.

Such an idea deserved a home in a book, but since no book existed, at least there must needs be a review. On the day before Christmas break, tucked under the box scores of the seminary basketball team, was my review of *The Relieved Paradox* by the elusive Professor Bibfeldt. I left school with a heavy vacation agenda. Officials had asked whether my fianceé, my parents, and I would discuss my undertaking an overseas assignment the next year. A small congregation of displaced Baltic people in London awaited a pastor. I already envisioned time at Covent Gardens or the British Museum. A telegram came: would I return to seminary a day early? A couple of professors had grown eager to see the Bibfeldt book, while others were equally suspicious about its existence.

What followed has never been completely revealed. In the world of Bibfeldt, not what happened but what everyone believes happened, matters. It was filtered to us that what we conceived as a satire on a system looked to some like the targeting of a professor or two who were walking parodies of the system. Since we could show that "all of us," not "some of us" were the victims, we were simply asked to cease and desist from further propagandizing the Bibfeldt lore. And after we could no longer publicize him, the good-natured victims of the hoax, forgiving all, began to quote him at us. Evidently it was decided, however, that the young candidate for London had proven himself to be too immature and irresponsible to represent the church so far away. He must be seasoned as an apprentice or curate under a salty senior minister.

Coming under that minister's influence was one of the great graces of my life. But one unwelcome hook was attached. The assistants in that parish were expected to continue work for the doctor of philosophy degree. This forced me to the graduate work that helped advance my one-and-the-many project. My story of a journey would sound more portentous were Bibfeldt to remain in the shadows. But he serves numerous functions. If our lives are guided, he helps prove that God works through apparent accidents. Second, he shows that the theologians—like gods—are easier to control if we invent them. (For example, I was trying earlier on these pages to get around the "jealous" God in order to produce a more manipulable and congenial one.) Further, Bibfeldt is a reminder that a person need not exist in order to influence lives; had his image not come along, I would be learning Latvian or Lithuanian. And since Bibfeldt was a satiric, not a comic creation, he shows that we believe—as satirists do—that this almost hopeless world is capable of being changed. If W. H. Auden is right, the comic mode, on the other hand, copes with a fated and never so malleable order.

Ordination: ever since those days we have heard people debating whether or not to ordain women and homosexuals, but most debaters slide right past one point. They know very little about what ordination is! I am not sure that clerical ordination means any empowerment that does not

come to all Christians at baptism. But since no one could
prescribe how to think of it, many of us regard it as
somehow ontological and sacramental. This meant that the
ministerial mandates and graces, to which we responded
with a vow, signaled a change in how things were put
together for us in the universe of meanings. In the present
journey, it also meant an attempt to combine the convictions
nurtured in an isolated tribe with ecumenical commitments
that kept emerging. The assistantship was creative but,
remember, I was also condemned to graduate school, first a
theological master's and then to doctoral work at the
University of Chicago.

Through the prep school years, that university had
served as a mecca for some of us hitchhikers. We would
crowd in on its guests, 'Great-Ideas' people like T.S. Eliot or
Jacques Maritain. It surprises me now to recall how little
culture shock there was after enrollment in a tradition we
were taught to find uncongenial. True, many theological
students at Chicago talked an arcane language of process
theology to which my kind found difficulty responding. But
gradually we recognized that almost everyone there was
from the provinces and parishes. Localism and tribalism
lived on, even in the kind of rebel student who tried to cover
his tracks with, "Ah was a Suth'n Babtist last year, but now
ah'm a Unitarian." If the divinity school offered some
vestigial shelter, the history department, my other home,
did not. Yet there, too, we found collegiality born of
responsiveness to the worlds of the people attracted to
its inquiries, or to the subject of those researches. The
combativeness of scholars seemed designed less to "do us
in" than competitive church life was; it was to "bring us out."
So, twenty-six years into life, for the first time I was at last on
soil where I could confront the subject matter of a life's
work.

The effort to confront traditions most remote from my

own led to a dissertation on the "Infidel," the anticlerical and antichurchly freethinker. Given the weakness of organized atheism and the dispersal of secularists in this nation, I assumed that villainous church people had successfully suppressed mention of their names and talents. But like so many historical inquiries, this led to a complete upsetting of presuppositions. The church in fact had been the main instrument of publicity for the feeble freethinking traditions in America, as they put these minor talents to major use for their own purposes. Today, though some of my best friends remain infidels, these findings mean less to me than does the recall of the terrain to which they led. Words like *pluralist, secular,* or *modern* became my chief intellectual preoccupations, even though my occupations took me for a time into safer areas. Still, after the Bibfeldt caper it was easy to be ready for anything, including what could have been new confinement between church walls and under a low chapel ceiling in the parish ministry.

2
Responsory:
The Parish Community

Under the title *The World and the Parish* her publisher gathered two large volumes of undergraduate writings by Willa Cather. To this novelist from the Great Plains, "the world" represented cosmopolitan concerns, while "the parish" symbolized the provincial. For seven years "the parish" for me meant a particular plot of ground in suburban Chicago, the home of a mission congregation. "The world" was visible through a window that an editorial post on the ecumenical weekly *The Christian Century* provided. While this dual vocation called for weekly commuting, and for constant mingling of different kinds of energies, I must reflect on the two experiences separately.

The world and the parish stand in some sort of tension for all who want to address both. Methodist founder John Wesley helped inaugurate a new era, the one we call modern, when he announced, "the world is my parish." No longer would arbitrary geographical limits confine his ministry as they had defined the ministries of his predecessors for the previous millennium. No longer would the community of believers be simply a collection of people who inherited the proper genes or who lived in the right place. Now ministers must go out and evoke a parish community anywhere in the world. For all the rude emotions his movements inspired, it was also a civilizing force. Christians gained a new view of a shrinking globe. They followed the ships of empire and came to know people unlike themselves.

Over against this universalizing impulse, modernity has also produced a counterforce. In order to wall off or at least to ward off many erosive aspects of these new worlds, believers often tended to become localist in mentality. Most of their energies and almost all of their imagination went back into the congregational forms of faith. They came to lack empathy for any fellow-believers who lived across the line they drew between suburb and ghetto. They did not care to interact between social classes, between northern and southern hemispheres, between black and white communities. One could almost hear any leader among them say, "my parish is the world," which meant, "the only world I care to know." The Germans speak of *Kirchturmgeschichte*, the reporting on church circumstances from the viewpoint of one's own church tower. Where the idea that a single parish is the whole world operates, members measure the called ministry only by local norms, not by whether or not the leaders help increase their responsiveness beyond parish boundaries.

To be pastor of the Church of the Holy Spirit in a most-provincial-minded church body and to be at the same time an editor of *The Christian Century* was a most vivid way of inducing a strain that at times could have become almost unbearable. Yet the members of the church generously

shared my calendar and they made it a point to take
seriously the viewpoints I brought back with me. The
editors of the magazine conscientiously kept me busy
bringing the parish agenda and outlook to their columns.
The good humor of senior counselors helped me cope with
the delicacy of the position. In 1957 a representative of a
European journal asked for a report on a world church
gathering from the viewpoint of one who has "one foot in
the parish of an antiecumenical denomination and the
other foot in the office of the ecumenical *The Christian
Century*." I consulted Chicago Professor Joseph Sittler about
the posture. He twinkled and said, "That seems to me to be
a pose guaranteed to produce a hernia!"

Therewith Sittler provided an eye-opening lead for the
report. But that anatomical image would never do in a staid
German theological journal. After consulting the dictionaries
for the most abstruse and thus most acceptable alternative to
it, I resolved to write "from an equilibristic stance." How
would the Germans translate it? Simple: *Balanzakt!*

A balance act on the tightrope is not a classic way of
making the Christian journey. The pilgrimage, the exodus,
or an exile promise more spiritual yield. Yet in many ways,
not all of them perverse, this form of movement serves as an
apt description for the modern condition. It meant
frequent tiltings from one side to the other, from the world
to the parish, from the ecumenical to the provincial, from
the universal to the denominational, from the global to the
tribal. Yet every time, one moved in the face of a danger
that to compensate *too* much for a tilt would bring a fall that
would end the whole act.

Though the Divinity School catalog back then advertised
that the Ph.D. was a good minimum preparation for the
pastoral ministry, the faculty seemed surprised when I took
its line seriously. During the last year of the doctoral studies
I found myself occasionally and mysteriously invited for

meals with passing-through university deans and college presidents. I knew so little about the process of being sounded out that it took some time to realize that they were not interested in my opinions over breakfast but in the possibility of my joining their faculties. In those late medieval days there were more academic posts than qualified Ph.D. prospects for them, a situation beyond comprehension today. My advisers had been lining up these interviews, each of which turned abruptly cool when over morning toast I would announce a firm resolve to return soon to the pastorate. That was one way for a Ph.D. to be dismissed as an eccentric. More recently the gulf between the world of academic intention and local parish service has narrowed considerably, and all for the better.

The preceding years of graduate work combined with brief interim pastorates, often in blue-collar or black parishes, had served to inspire an interest in my helping form a new parish, there better to learn how community develops. Could my stubborn pastoral resolve have been born of the conceit of a budding historian? Through two centuries, before and after the rise of the modern university, which became the site for advanced religious thought, the people I regarded as the most creative public religious thinkers had spent all their careers or at least many of their earlier years in the pastorate. All of them credited their members with having fired their vision, even if the demands of parishioners also helped generate the frustrations that come with workaday life.

At the head of this company was Jonathan Edwards. He was not only the most notable local minister in the First Great Awakening, a man who worked the home front in a Massachusetts parish while the more flamboyant revivalists took to the road. His was also as fine a philosophical mind as the American religious community has yet seen. After the Northamptonites ran him out, Edwards spent several more pastoral years with the Indians at Stockbridge. Amid the odors of their bear grease he repreached incomprehensible sermons. Then he would hole himself up in a tiny cabin to write his treatises. At the end he became president of the College of New Jersey at Princeton; whereupon he died. Edwards carried on a career-long balancing act. He could mingle great calls for a "concert of prayer" among the nations and the writing of cosmic sermons on *The History of the Work of Redemption* with pastoral duties and minute psychological scrutiny of his parishioners.

Horace Bushnell, a century later, lived in a time that offered him more academic opportunity because there were more seminaries and colleges, but he elected to spend his life at a church in Hartford, Connecticut. His was a new urban milieu. He watched revivalist fires burn out whole districts and then burn out personalities. From his parochial vantage what was necessary, he thought, was *Christian nurture*. From there he also provided a public theology in support of the Union, though its militant tone needed tempering by Abraham Lincoln. From the local congregation base Bushnell devised a theory of language that still merits scholarly exploration.

At the turn of the present century a new environment and new problems emerged. When the social gospel came to address the needs of industrial America, there rose a prophet named Walter Rauschenbusch, the third figure to be chipped into my figurative theological Mount Rushmore. In the later years of his deafness he was to become a teacher of church history at Rochester. But he gained his lifelong social vision during eleven years at Second Baptist Church in a slummy sector of New York's west side. They called it Hell's Kitchen for good reasons. There he worked among German immigrants, who were almost lost in the ethnic mix. Handicapped though Rauschenbusch was by ill health and distracted though he seemed to be by his sense of reserve and an urge to pursue studies in Germany, his parishioners knew that they held highest priority in his concern. The butcher who spoke for them all at their pastor's farewell eloquently expressed common gratitude for his responsiveness and fidelity. As for tightrope walking: somehow Rauschenbusch could draw magnate John D. Rockefeller to the muddy gutters of Hell's Kitchen in order to gain support for slum work at the very time when the preacher was proclaiming a view of the kingdom of God that would subvert the system in which Rockefeller was the most visible figure.

In the 1920s, Reinhold Niebuhr spent thirteen years between graduate studies at Yale and a career at New York's Union Theological Seminary in a conventional small parish in Detroit. To carry the provincial motif further: just as Rauschenbusch had come from outside the mainstream, from the ethnic and ecclesiatical backwaters of the German Baptists, so Niebuhr emerged from a German Reformed and Evangelical context that was not in the main Protestant channel. While Reinhold's mind may not have matched his own brother's for theological depth, his also displayed power and scope. No one could accuse Niebuhr of having turned merely provincial because he was so long parochial. All his life he insisted that his academic public theology derived first from his day-to-day work in Detroit in an age of industrial conflict and middle-class aspiration. In his theology he fused a reading of the Bible and Marx and Dewey on one hand with a reading of the faces of ordinary Detroiters on the other.

Since there are only four spaces on Mount Rushmore, I can now without blushing make clear that these figures were only exemplars for a historically minded young minister who, before he began, saw the canon closed on their kind. Such models did provide a template for people like me to impose on our ministry. The heirs of the

awakened people of the era of Edwards or the descendants
of Bushnell's nurtured ones were still around in abundant
supply. The victims and agents of immigrant and industrial
change from the era of Rauschenbusch and Niebuhr also
had millions of counterparts. But a new milieu was now
taking bemusing form. In the 1950s two fields were
especially problematic. One was the inner city, not yet then
often called the ghetto. To black and white ministers alike
this zone offered special promise and danger and for a few
years attracted the energies of white seminarians. My
interim and ad hoc ministries in such situations bred a taste
for the scene but they also revealed no special competencies
for the role.

The call that I did not seek took me to the other zone,
middle-class suburbia. One-third to one-half of the largely
white population was relocating on that frontier within
hardly more than a decade. After a generation it is not
possible for me to recall the sense of venture which that
frontier implied without recapturing some of the defensive
spirit ministers like me were then called to summon. To have
left a secular graduate school for a mission in an African leper
colony, an urban night-ministry to jazz musicians, or a college
chaplaincy, would have been so natural that no one would
have questioned it. But in the 1950s to join a migration to
mass-produced suburban settings looked to critics less like
mission than betrayal, less like Christian work than capitalist
competition, less like a possible extension of the church than
like exile into the wilderness.

Not without some warrant, critics saw the new suburbs
to be evasions of urban chaos. Academic sociologists with
considerable conformity decried the conformity of the
suburban life. In those years when ex-GI's and their
as-yet-unliberated spouses were eager to settle down and
contribute to the baby boom, real estate and mortgage
practices consistently drove them to have to buy new houses

beyond the genteel old suburbs. Their attackers simply dismissed these people as look-alikes in cookie-cutter and ticky-tacky towns. Certainly they merited no ministry and were not candidates for legitimate human service. At last God had created a class of people who were supposed to be beyond the scope of love.

Few of the stereotypes were of any use for dealing with people who became and remain as good friends as I have ever met. Curiously, I knew some of them already from having visited their campuses a couple of years before. These alumni, scorned by the academy, were themselves the products of the academic scorners. Either they had learned little at the universities or the critics were overlooking something in them or mere economic necessity and cultural pressures must have been forming a new brand of people out of them as postgraduates. To me the residents never made up a laboratory. Instead we started a ministry. They were as highly varied a set of people as one could meet in the inner city, the old style suburb, town and country, or even most ivied campus enclaves. They settled on what had been a pasture west of O'Hare International Airport. Within seven years the new village grew from no population to a score of thousands. If I instinctively resented the doorbell-pushing, some of the committee meetings—I am not at home in administration—or the task of helping plan and erect two buildings, I came to marvel over the generosity of these laypeople. After a twelve-hour day, including commuting time, they found energies to work for and, more and more, through the parish. Mortgaged beyond the bounds of reason, many of them still tithed. Drained by the demands of their employers, they sustained imagination for parish life.

While the idea that "my [own] parish is the world" is both imperial and confining, to the alert pastor any congregation can offer sufficient variety to warrant one's calling it a

window on the world. Were our members and their
neighbors really so much like each other? To the airline
passenger flying from the west to land at O'Hare the lineup
of the streets and the architecture of the houses in such
towns must have hinted at diminished human variety, as do
the condominiums of a newer urban scene. The first year of
life in that instant community, however, called forth all that
or more than I had learned about counseling in the
aftermaths of crises. These involved, among others, dealing
with rape, suicide, murder, abortion when it was simply
illegal, homosexuality when it was unrecognized by Christians, alcoholism as a contagious disease, child abuse, incest,
and embezzlement, and yes, there were also utterly normal
people—like their minister!

As for the varieties of organized religious life, many
innovations and experiments occurred in parishes in that
decade. A decade later it was puzzling to me to find a new
generation shopping for alternatives among Eastern religious imports. In what truly *were* look-alike and cookie-cutter settings, the adherents sat in contrived and churning
silence for ten hours. Yet they claimed that they found an
hour of even high-intensity Christian worship boring. For
the intellectual-minded seminarian who dismissed the
parish as an arena for thinkers, I would pose what is a
constant situation for ministers, What do you say and do
when you are called upon to help a young mother come to
terms with terminal disease and to help her family
thereafter? Ministers use up more theodicy in a season in
those circumstances than they would in a decade of
classroom theology.

No one can describe the parish journey without finding,
at many turns along the way, the need to recall the horrors
alongside the glories. A random snapshot: a young wife in
the parish had problems relating sexually to her husband.
Though she was in the medical profession and was highly

informed about the physical aspects of sex, something blocked her involvement with her mate. You were called in as a counselor at the side of medical people. By amazing coincidence, it turned out that you knew her father well, back in the city. You always thought much of him and decided to exploit the tie, should the counseling turn a bit less nondirective. Conversations about him might provide a bond and eventually a base for the daughter's self-understanding and a first step toward therapy. But for reasons you did not understand, this course led nowhere at all. Suddenly she blurted out a reason for you to comprehend: "You don't understand *anything*, pastor. You think so much of my father. You think he's part of the solution. You're wrong. I know him better. I know him very intimately. He's nothing but a goddam incestuous bastard."

On such days, you mentally pick yourself up, though you have been trained never to raise a nondirective eyebrow, and you scurry back in thought to the texts that did not prepare you for what must next be heard or said. Nothing so dramatic as this is likely to happen until the next session with someone else—an hour or two from now. You understand at last why teachers of counseling prescribe so much listening. You have a great deal to be silent about. But in such encounters you also find that the parish, a world of miseries and incestuous bastard fathers, houses human varieties that the similarities in architecture and street design obscure but never remove.

For relating the parish and the world, the suburban pastor counselor was likely to hear searching criticisms of capitalist demands and the merchandising ethos. They did not come from the trendy campus Marxist that each college found then and still finds it advisable to include in its mix. Instead you would hear them voiced by young couples whose marriages strained under the pressures of Sunday-night-to-Friday-night jet-age-travel schedules by salespeople. Such ministers were also likely to discover measures of altruism that no theory of "the selfish gene" would simply explain. They discerned a sense of the presence of God among people there as readily as in the more faddish ashrams.

They say you can kill a person with an apartment as well as with a gun—it merely takes a bit longer. America was also killing young families with suburban houses. Yet from under those roofs came people who had insight into their condition and at least some clues as to what to do about it. Be it also said, most of them likewise found innumerable occasions of joy. Many of these came amid what to distant critics were the trivia of existence but what amounted to the heart of living: at christenings and marriages, in movements of creative achievement, in the minor triumphs of a younger generation, when breaches or bodies were healed, or in affirmations over cold cuts and coffee after a graveside trek.

No one gifted with synoptic vision or total recall would simply romanticize the new middle-class forms of life after the American midcentury. But eleven years of parish ministry and especially seven in the mission congregation have ever after made it impossible for me simply to purchase into the real denunciations that are parts of many kinds of Liberation Theology. I know what side I would be on in most Latin American countries, and the same totalist furies that move revolutionaries would course through me. But at any distance from their wars one must also learn the importance of making distinctions. Any neat division of worlds into the oppressing and the oppressed derives too much from a mere glance at the physical circumstances of life.

Yes, we suburbanites "had" more than did ghetto dwellers or Chilean peasants, though what we had was not necessarily more security then tenured-faculty critics possessed. And our possessing may have obscured some of our vision of human need elsewhere, though parishes like ours were at least agencies for bringing distant and closeup worlds together—as almost nothing else was then doing. Some of what the liberationists wanted for the poor was more "having" of the sort that produced spiritual problems in the world of relative affluence. Few of the new burgeoning middle class of people, for all their shortsightednesses and prejudices—which they held in a measure that compares to those held by ghetto dwellers, Chilean peasants, and academic critics, we must presume—could be described as utterly unoppressed.

Why must it hurt to write lines like these? They leave one vulnerable to the charge of insensitivity and a lack of social passion during the very effort to be honest about the demonic in all human existence, in the very attempt to be a faithful reporter. They prevent one for a moment from keeping up a strident pitch of prophetic denunciation against egregious injustices. But they do not rise from blindness over the differences in the worlds of relative "haves" and absolute "have nots," as if one lacked sympathy for people in real physical and political misery. Here as so often one must appeal to a line of Rousseau: you can expect my thoughts to be consistent with one another, but you cannot expect me to assert them all at once. On another day, in another context, it will be just as necessary to speak up for some other dimensions of Liberation Theology and to chide comfortable America for its lack of identifications.

This day, at this point in a remembered journey, it is important to say that in the eyes of one parishioner in any parish one can see a whole world. In any such situation the message that Christ brings deliverance to the captives is urgent. We have looked and seen, behind the bravado and self-assurance of a man, the wounded heart of all people. In the visage of a sullen and self-hating alcoholic woman one recognizes a torment no different from that which the

demons stir anywhere and any time. In an age of home-
building and home buying one could also discern what
Martin Buber meant when he talked of "an epoch of
homelessness," a void in the heart that inflicts its damage as
much in an American suburb as among the displaced in the
Sudan.

Selfishness is selfishness wherever it appears, even in the
spiritual life and in the central act of parish existence,
worship. The leader must often look out and recognize
what Psalm 106:12-15a diagnosed. After the Lord saved
"our fathers in Egypt,"

> Then they believed his words;
>   they sang his praise.
> But they soon forgot his works;
>   they did not wait for his counsel.
> But they had a wanton craving in the wilderness,
>   and put God to the test in the desert;
> he gave them what they asked,
>   but sent leanness into their soul. (verse 15b KJV)

The last line of this special translation for he "sent a wasting
disease among them" indicates what a worship leader
noticed on many days when he looked into the parish
mirror. We had what we asked for and then we got leanness
in our souls.

Our simple chapel followed the architectural model of
"the tent for the people of God on the march." As a
community we grew because the situation was right for
growth. Behind every story of parish success there is a story
of ready circumstances. A ministerial contemporary in the
evangelically catholic tradition attended a church growth
workshop and came home to push three thousand
doorbells in overchurched fundamentalist territory. He
gained three prospects and one member. He nursed
"failure ulcers" while I faced "success ulcers," despite our
equal competence but because of different settings.

The surveyors of population told us that 16.9 percent of the new arrivals to our community were by background of our communion. We found the background often to be remote, consisting of little more than occasional pit stops at Sunday school twenty years before. But these migrants did provide a cohort on which to draw, and we more than made up for our failure to attract from that flank. Many of our people had previously been wholly uncommitted, self-styled raw pagans, or restless church-shoppers. It may be that one does learn less about the nature of "the world" over against "the parish" from rapid growth situations than in more discouraging locales. They can easily mislead.

Always in the back of my mind was the remembrance of those confining walls and low ceilings at St. Paul's. Did we do as well as its elders at nurturing group loyalty, at building up the tribe? The task was made difficult by the variety of members and their great mobility. Did we do better now than the St. Pauls of the world to help people combine loyalty to their House of Muumbi with responsiveness to others—a task that, after all, was at the center of a life-work?

Let me disabuse anyone who thinks that a rootless and mobile population by nature is exempt from the prejudices that make for uncivil tribalism. It is precisely among such citizens that the meaner sorts of fundamentalists have their greatest successes. Where identities are hard to come by and where erosion works its boldest effect, people are fair game for those who come at them with absolutist authority and totalist styles of group life. There people build the thickest walls and seek the greatest social distances.

Those tendencies were not as pronounced in the fifties as they are today, but the dangers were there. While suburbanites derided the traditionalism of their elders at church back in town, we soon learned to be careful with innovations. Anything done two years in a row became an instant tradition and was hard to reform. While the days of "the true visible church on earth" were hard to re-create, some members at least brought with them states of mind that could easily distance them from other sectors of the Christian church. But we kept experimenting with ways to inspire fidelity while combining it with openness.

Not everything was in our favor, even in that era of good feelings. The most liberal Protestants back then had to discipline themselves to policies of comity—to restrain themselves from converging on the greenest pastures for missions. That was a translation for "places that could pay returns on investments quickly." Mission pastors were sent out to compete with one another. Graced as we were with the company of congenial colleagues and benign neigh- boring parishioners, we all still noticed how easy it was to fall into the "I am of Apollos" versus "I am of Cephas" business. Yet many gestures countered it. The Second Vatican Council had not yet allowed for Catholic openness, but the priest from next door—our church lawns adjoined each other—a man of unmovably conservative instincts who had an expansive spirit, pushed all rules to their bounds. Some mornings before Pope John gave encouragement to such activities, I would find Father Morrison in silent prayer in our sanctuary. Prayers for the Marty boys, who needed all the praying they could get, were staples at Christmas Eve Mass next door. What is hard to puzzle out is the fact that we allowed ourselves to be Christian in the biblical sense only to the degree that we strained at our own church rules, when we tried to transcend mere personal friendliness and translate it into spiritual bonding.

What became clear to many of the competitors of that era was that we were working with an image of God that itself remained tribalist. God was a predator who sent us out to do preying. Though the divine is boundless, we were in a boundary-building profession in the name of God. The only way to assure that we could combine conviction with responsiveness was to enlarge and deepen our experience of God. For us in that generation this meant taking part in a spiritual journey that kept worship central in congregational life.

Sometimes along a journey the companions must unburden themselves to one another. Let me here and now. The parish effort induced a conclusion about myself that may have little bearing on the journey of some others and may even lead a few to turn off at this point. The confession might suggest leanness in my soul, or a mere indication of a personal style. In any case, twenty subsequent years of spiritual hitchhiking on the meditations and mysticisms of others, especially the desert fathers, the contemplative mothers, or the hermits, led me to a realization: solitary prayer is not the most creative access to the experience of God for some of us.

Efforts to improve this situation through spiritual disciplines have had little effect. We have *wu wei*-ed and breathed deeply, fasted or meditated transcendentally and immanentally, practiced bodily disciplines and attempted spiritual transport. We have plundered the lore of East and West and have tried to latch on to southern hemispheric pieties in order to supplement our provincially northern instincts. The whole library of past prayer is available, and some of us have- even dared to be projected into envisionings of the future of piety. We have prayed to learn to pray well alone and then tried techniques of letting go and not caring—in the prospect that something might thus happen. We have been with Brother Lawrence in the kitchen, seeking a sense of the presence of God among the pots and pans. There have been times when some have even been positioned like Bernini's sculpted Teresa of Avila, in whom the eros of union with the divine comes as with the force of orgasm.

To little effect! Some day, some way, where it is un-expected and perhaps where not sought, such a solitary enthusiasm might ignite itself. There have been glimpses and glimmers, some of them bright enough to provide a sense of identity with the achievers but hardly promising enough to inspire some search down certain paths. Do we resist for reasons of which we cannot be aware? Have we not placed a sufficiently high premium on the search in isolation, the lonely inward journey? Might it be that we often find ourselves repelled by much babble and chatter about intimacy with a chummy God, or repulsed by commercialized how-to ventures that mechanize the pro-cess? Are we too secular? As Nazi-victim Father Delp asked, Could it be that somewhere along the way a portion of humanity strayed beyond a hitherto forbidden horizon, to a terrain where God has chosen to be absent? Have we set a priori limits on what is allowable in such an experience, thanks to academic skepticism? Did we set those bounds so high for others that, in Peter Berger's terms, they had to "smuggle in the gods in plain brown wrappers"—hence the exotic character of so much of the modern search? Does the truly religious chord strike no response in our unmusical hearts?

During the parish years it became necessary to inquire intensely about such subjects and to come to some reso-lutions. Certainly we had friends and heroes who translated solitary experience into lives of quality. Once on a television program in the season when it was fashionable to talk of the death of God, an interviewer asked Rabbi Abraham Joshua Heschel if he thought God was dead. Heschel jumped up, oblivious to the camera, knocking coffee over the rest of us: "Oh, no! God is alive! I am not sure you and you and you are present, but God is. God is more near to us than we are to ourselves." A couple of years later Heschel was leading us into the streets to witness for racial justice and peace.

Thomas Merton was another persuader, because his journey occurred against the background of agonies. Yet, though his was confined to a monastic retreat and even a hermitage, he transferred his soul's torment into a vision of justice. Later he was to say that his whole life followed a simple trajectory. Whatever Merton had written or said, it could all be reduced to one truth: that God calls persons to union with himself and with one another in Christ. This same monk transacted with the fire in his soul until he saw visions of concentration camps wherein white America would sequester black Americans, or of great bombs that would ruin Vietnam. So extreme were his envisionings, so strident his words, that I felt moved to chide him in print and he responded in kind. Yet a few seasons later it became necessary to apologize to him; his seeing had been more accurate than mine. The fires burned, in the cities of America and the fields of Vietnam.

Despite the record of geniuses like Heschel and Merton, in many others the search for God meant a search for the self in isolation. For them the inward journey meant escape from the world of external necessity. The modern charismatic movement, for all its promise, is vulnerable to such tendencies. I have observed it with special care because before the pentecostal movement erupted in mainline Christianity, I had dedicated my ministry—both through a master's thesis topic and through the name of our Church of the Holy Spirit—to the Holy Spirit. But after the charismatic outbreak we were often told that we did not "have" the Holy Spirit because we did not cultivate certain pieties. The movement can boast its own counterparts to Heschel and Merton, particularly in the southern hemisphere, and more may emerge in our own. But too many of those who took out a patent on their way of having the Holy

Spirit only repelled others from this form of search. If the tendency to spiritual narcissism is present in that most green tree of Christian charismata, it has come to be even more true in the dry. Among these latter are campus-based pop mysticisms, which rely on imports from the East packed for weekend retreat dosages.

Those parish years also inspired a reservation against too much devotion to one form of the journey. Friedrich Heiler distinguished between purely mystical and prophetic prayer. Mystical prayer had its roots in the yearning of the devout person for union with the infinite, while prophetic prayer arose from the profound need of the heart and the longing for grace. Mystical prayer demanded artificial preparation through refined psychological techniques of meditation while prophetic petition broke forth more spontaneously. Mystical prayer meant a kind of weary climbing by degrees to the heights of the divine vision and union with God, while prophetic prayer was a stormy assault upon the heart of God.

While invoking Heiler we have to reinvoke Rousseau: the distinction between the two kinds of devotion is not as sharp. To speak up for the prophetic is not to demean all forms of the mystical. But it was important in our parish worship to discern our own genius in the light of our tradition before relating to others. George Santayana somewhere drew a line between kinds of mysticisms that seek union with God on God's level versus kinds of spirituality that seek union with God on a human level. The latter squared with an insight from Martin Luther's stab at defining theology, based on Exodus 33:20-23. Moses on Sinai wanted to see the glory of God face to face, to have union on the divine level. No, "you cannot see my face; for man shall not see me and live." The Lord would only hide Moses in the cleft of a rock and there would cover him, while the divine glory passed by. "Then I shall take away my hand, and you shall see my back; but my face shall not be seen."

With a fine Hebraic-German sense of the vulgarly appropriate, Luther seized on this concept of the back of God, the *posteriora dei,* and said that only that person who was content with a view of the hind parts of God could be considered a theologian. This approach opposes a theology of glory, beholding or contemplation that tried to move beyond the posterior of God or the underside of history seen in Jesus Christ in the theology of the cross. To cherish another approach was to make a claim upon God ("I found it!") and thus, for fallible humans, to seek an insecure basis for a relation that should get its guarantee from divine initiative and grace. Not being as busy with Luther's battle in a day when the experience of God in any form is difficult, we tried to be responsive to mystics and glory-folk. But we did not want these sunny beholders of the vision of God to dismiss as invalid those of us who, in the private journey, were more afflicted with or addicted to what Karl Rahner called "a wintry form of spirituality."

For us, God was to be found in the assembly, the Q'hal Yahweh or congregation of the Lord. Dietrich Bonhoeffer's word that Jesus Christ exists *as* congregation struck with special resonance during our common search. The travelers made room for a combusting experience of God, but as parishioners they reported that it came more likely through the shared Lord's Supper, the traumatic joy that accompanies the baptisms of the the Easter vigil, that bonds young people around campfire vespers or in matins when dawn breaks at a work camp. The impact of the prayer of the church reached us on days when mystical assent could not. Intercessory prayer, "loving one's neighbors on one's knees," bore a mark of authenticity that self-centered petitions often lacked. "Response" became

the root word in understanding worship, an awareness that
I was privileged to emphasize when naming a national
journal of music, worship, and the arts, *Response.*

Two elements from the morning or matins service
described the outreach and insearch of parish life. One was
the Invitatory, with which one begins the day:

> O come, let us sing to the Lord; . . .
> Let us come into his presence with thanksgiving . . . .
>
> (Ps. 95:1-2a)

Just as worship took its note from the Invitatory, so all the
congregation had to be inviting. This concept is at the root
of that evangelism which tries to move beyond the concept
of a stalking god who sends out people to pounce on the
unconverted. Psychiatrist Robert Coles has urged that in
the Christian gathering people seek a sense of the presence
of God first of all. It is at the heart of the motion called the
Invitatory.

In return, the people say the Responsory, and we liked to
think of the congregation as a responsory personified and
made communal. God speaks and the gathering responds
in the form of a counterpledge, a reply to the promise. A
sculpture at the entrance to the little Church of the Holy
Spirit was a constant reminder. On it were the words of
Martin Luther at the dedication of the Torgau Chapel, the
first church built for our communion: "Nothing should
ever happen here except that our dear Lord speak to us
through his holy word and we, in turn, respond with
prayers and hymns."

Pause. Where exactly have we been taking the companions along this journey? We set out to talk about helping
tribalists turn civil and cosmopolitans come to conviction.
We began worrying about a violent world in which religion
reinforced the massive convulsive ingatherings of people

against other groups. And now we end up talking about a plaque on the wall of a mission in the docile suburbs. We promised to talk about commitment in a world of the spiritually passive and now we divert ourselves from the passion of the private question to line up with the congregations uttering Responsories to Invitatories, as if liturgical elements set the terms for anything that mattered in the real world. Certainly this is only a diversion, an aesthetic stop at a quaint roadside shrine.

And yet. . . . And yet . . . .

Romano Guardini liked to say that worship was *zwecklos aber doch sinnvoll,* "pointless but significant." Worship is pointless on the agenda of grimly productive believers, those computers with legs who believe that bureaucracy saves and pronouncements heal. Or of dour revolutionaries whose private utopias, they think, will rise on the ashes of past prayer and obsolete forms of human bondings.

Corporate worship was central to the parish and became an agent of our natural doing in the world. The years that were to come, now remembered simply as the Sixties, provided a test for thousands of parishes. What became ever more clear in those years of social activism was that the church in the world has no power except the kind generated through shared prayer, common symbols, communal belief, and corporate purpose. Those Christians who acted as if they could live entirely off a spiritual capital in which others had invested quickly expended all the resources and lost their power. Where are they now? What has become of them? Half-believers or other-believers who heard their appeals were free to respond by engaging in creative foot-dragging or Sunday soldiering. When they were faced with calls that they did not understand or believe in, these voluntary troops disappeared. The church can coerce no armies or revenues; it cannot imprison or detain dissidents.

Where critics and doers did live off shared prayer, they kept being spiritually replenished. Heschel and Merton were two examples of this, but others across the spectrum of right to left among those who uttered their Responsory also set out to change the world. Dorothy Day, a woman of endurance who lasted through many decades without ever becoming fashionable, kept working away at the ideal of *The Catholic Worker* on the basis of a piety nurtured on the pre-Vatican II Mass. She could never quite understand why fugitive Father Daniel Berrigan wanted to use real-looking bread and an earthen chalice. Christ had been present for her in the little plastic-looking discs and the silver chalice of the priest. As for Berrigan, when he was not being a productive activist he was likely to be engaged in pointless but significant acts like praying the Psalms, teaching the Scripture or, for God's sake, writing poetry. Aleksandr Solzhenitsyn drew sticks for the fire of his dissent from the tradition of Orthodox piety and worship. Martin Luther King, Jr., remained ever at home in the black Baptist worship that in his father's congregation and in his own shaped him to change the world.

For the congregation as Responsory, reply takes the form of spirituality materialized. Charles Peguy once cried that everything began in mysticism and ended in politics. Here mysticism means communion with God in common worship and politics means all kinds of action in the *polis,* the human city. To dwell on Peguy: for him, to raise oneself to the eternal, it was not enough to depreciate the temporal. To raise oneself to grace—and this "raising" derives from the language of mystical assent—it was never enough to depreciate the world. People believed, he charged, that because they lacked the strength and the grace to belong to nature, they belonged to grace. Because they lacked temporal courage, they believed they had passed the threshold of the eternal. Because they did not have the boldness to be worldly, they considered themselves to be on the side of God. Not belonging to humans, they believed they belonged to God. Because they loved nobody, they believed they loved God. And yet Jesus Christ, the meeting point of Invitatory and Responsory, was human.

Being itself a Responsory—if we may now personify the action of worship—did not mean that a congregation must be a weather vane to turn with every wind or an agent trying to be relevant to everything. Just the opposite. The responding self *is* a self; the responsory congregation has an identity. I like to speak of it as having a genius or, better, a "core," just as a fulfilled person has a core. (For the punster, the Latin word for heart is *cor*). The core is the part of the fruit in which one finds the seed for the future. In the foundry, the core at the heart of an object assures strength for its filigreed extensions. The members always worship at their particular place and time, where they have to discern their own genius and mission. They then develop enough sense of inner sameness and continuity to match the same qualities in others. Then they can be committed without lapsing into anticivil tribalism.

From the middle of the parish years, my first published book, *The New Shape of American Religion* was, in its first half, a pessimistic look at what later came to be called civil religion. The second half was a hopeful treatment of the local congregation as a place whence one might undertake a task of renewal.

Some critics called this notion an example of "morphological fundamentalism." Not that I had been insufficiently critical of parishes as they were, nor that I expected of them more than an undertaking, a beginning, of reform. The issue was whether *any* hope for the parish was not a too uncritical attachment to the *morphé*, the very form of local cells.

Through thin and thick, as in the later *The Death and Birth of Parish* and a hundred magazine articles, I have lingered with the possibilities of the local congregation. Yes, there was room for hope in "emerging viable structures for ministry," as they were once called. But few emerged, almost none stayed viable, and most were structural designs rather than personal arenas. Yet the local congregation, which itself desperately needs experiment, survives. For a time it looked as if a spirit of reaction against remote agencies and bureaucracies would assure security to local communities of faith. But by the seventies they faced new problems.

On the one hand, many civil-minded churches of the mainline became demoralized. In a jugularly competitive market they wearied of aggression. They failed to win new members to replace those who relocated in retirement, fell away as youth, or died. Others, despite surveys to the contrary, believing they were losing because they had held controversial convictions in the sixties, withdrew and lost a sense of mission. Not all learned how to minister to hungers for the sense of the presence of God. Still others lost passion and settled for low levels of commitment.

Also since mid-century many of the convinced, vice versa, became belligerents instead of responsory bodies. A sudden shift in the *Zeitgeist,* the spirit of the times, led to the desertion by many of the ecumenical ideal. Their burgeoning congregation belonged to Apollos against Cephas or to Cephas against Paul. Tacticians read books that showed how in its mean mood, a public craved authoritarianism as a means to reinforce weak egos and shore up vague identities. Many wanted thick fortress walls both against signals from without and to keep their own within. They erected mirrors to help sustain the illusion that "my parish is the world" instead of windows to connect the parish to the world. Some raided other congregations for recruits and called it evangelism. They negatively valued all pieties other than their own and called it success. The tribes turned tribalistic, the committed lacked civility.

Both styles have since come to recognize still another threat, one that undercuts the whole idea of a responsory community. In the newest unfolding, only solitary individual experiences on isolated spiritual "trips" matter in the religious journey. Increasingly the mass media treat congregations as kindergartens of faith. They make heroes and heroines of the members of alumni associations of the congregations. "Of course, Celebrity X no longer attends the local Baptist church. She is 'into'. . . . this or that." Young people who discovered that mother was not the only cook took their religious search to the most exotic kitchens. The tendency developed to generate as many religions as there were persons. Each individual passed down a cafeteria line to dish up a plattered blend of, for example, a bit of remembered Catholicism, a dose of Judaism acquired from a shed spouse or a book of Buber, a mind-expansion gained from mild drugs, a whisp of Zen imported from a retreat, a touch of Jesus, a dab of Buddha, a new technique of meditation, a burp from macrobiotic diets, and a spurt from jogging—and called it a living faith. Do I have to add that it *is* possible for an American to sustain a lifelong serious journey by probing to their depths the works and ways of, say, an Eastern faith? That is different from eclecticism in things spiritual.

During the often thoughtless institutional religious boom of the fifties, congregations were taught that the enemy was secularism. The foe instead has turned out to be utterly private faith. Parishioners always knew that each of them must believe for themselves, but they were not to conceive of faith as a private invention of do-it-yourself entrepreneurs. Modernity did not see religion die; it was instead merely relocated. The world did not dismiss spirituality but saw it diffused. Father John Courtney Murray used to speak of the church as a Thing. One had to reckon with it, because it had condemning and saving power. Modernity so refines and grinds down religion that it can take no shape in anything that would scandalize or save others.

A couple hundred thousand exceptions remain. But no one who cherishes the responsory congregation can relax in the presence of faith that wants specific substance out of religion—be it success, healing, or a "high." When religion becomes a purely private affair, celebrities gather ephemeral clienteles while durable congregations wane.

The viewer or reader forms a one-to-one relation to a broadcaster or author and makes no commitment beyond the instant appeal of the purveyor. Each knows the maxim, "You are only as good as your last act." So each last act has to be more sensational than the one that went before. When leaders of such clienteles do stir their followers into making public forays, these are usually raids against some perceived conspirators against their empires—the pornographers, the homosexuals, the gamblers, the writers of evolution textbooks. They are rarely open engagements with those who would like to feed the world or bring measures of justice to it.

Hans Küng has written that the church begins not with a pious individual but with God. The pious individual alone could never achieve the transforming of isolated sinful persons into the people of God. An atomized crowd of pious individuals could never be a home for the homeless and isolated persons of today. Jesus Christ, existing as community, as congregation, is known in the response of gathered people who make up the body of which he is head. Those who commune on such terms need never turn tribalistic or predatory. They know the intrinsic value of worship and congregating, from whence they sit or kneel or whence they walk. Their successes will not lead to pride or their failures to despair. Seven years with a vital parish, and yet one so ordinary, provided lessons to carry along. I keep learning them still, having left the parish ministry, but never the parish and its world.

3

Responses:
The Ecumenical World

"One foot in the parish and the other foot in *The Christian Century*. . . ." Did that posture produce a hernia, or did that balancing act end in a fall? Certainly, there were strains between the daylight parish and the moonlight editing worlds. The parish was nonliberal in ethos, the magazine liberal. The parishioners did not see that the future kingdom of God depended upon their efforts, but responded on intrinsic terms. The ecumenical journal, on the other hand, had roots in the liberal concept of agency and carried in its genetic programming a theology to match. With tinges of regret and a brace of joyful realism I observe that almost twenty-five years later that ethos has been compromised if it has not disappeared. But in the twilight years there were enough traces to cause clash.

Charles Clayton Morrison, who purchased a dying magazine in 1908 was thought of as its founder. For decades he used its pages to propound his version of the social gospel, liberal theology, and a distinctive ecumenical pattern. Before the great wars he led Protestant pacifist forces and during the wars fought totalitarianism reluctantly, as a tragic necessity. After the wars he supported the League of Nations, the United Nations, and agencies to promote peace.

His cosmopolitanism had limits. To his enemies he was the quintessential WASP who was always wondering why the world did not conform to his genteel tradition. Though a pioneer in interfaith affairs, he was a victim of his place and time. Thus he drew from his contacts with American Jews, the leaders of Reform, an assimilationist model— "why can't everybody be like us?" With most of them in those days he was a non-Zionist, even an anti-Zionist. When they at last changed, he remained a critic of Israel. Five years before I joined the staff, *Century* editorials also described pluralism as "a national menace," while I was a champion of pluralism. Morrison was for racial integration. But like many social gospel figures he instinctively made Anglo-Saxon values normative. Novelist James Baldwin later asked of his kind, "Are you sure I want to be integrated into a burning house?" Morrison would have had no answer because the question was beyond him.

One could point to such flaws or limited contexts in any figure from the past. They all had the misfortune not to be born in our enlightened era and thus not to be in possession of all hindsights. To point to Morrison's follies detracts notice from his abilities, achievements, and charms. He brought excitement to the scene of religious journalism, enjoyed conflict as an instrument of the search for truth, and stirred otherwise lethargic and demoralized religious leaders to new vision and action. That sounds like an honorary degree citation, but behind cliché I recall him as an embodiment of such virtues.

Flesh and blood he was, an almost naïve fighter for his truths as if they were the only truths. He verged on being a liberal tribalist, his magazine being his House of Muumbi. Were he asked to rank church bodies, my antiecumenical one would have to rank near the bottom. He was friendly to me despite a theological gulf. But there were limits.

Dr. Morrison had as fine a sense of the Corinthian question, "Is Christ divided?" as anyone alive. And his sense of what to do about it was as compromised as everyone else's. In his case, "the unfinished reformation" meant a reunion of the Western non-, and in those days, anti-Roman Catholic churches. He had helped devise the Greenwich Plan to hasten and effect a union of mainline Protestant churches that would no longer wait for anyone else in Christendom.

Some fifty years after he acquired the magazine and long after he had holdings in it or hold on it, Morrison had not given up on the dream of reshaping the world through it—liberals, progressives, and optimists like he never could give up. That he had become virtually blind did not limit his getting around. He could come to the office if the occasion demanded it, with long editorials in huge handwriting on yellow pads. One day occasion demanded. He came storming off the elevator into the offices, his nostrils flaring and his eyes bright as if he could really see us: "Who wrote this week's editorial about Eastern Orthodoxy?"

Two of us confessed. To a man well into his nineties we were the "two young fellows."

"Don't you young fellows know what that kind of thinking will do to the ecumenical movement? How can you square that with the Greenwich Plan?"

Honestly, we had not asked the second question, though we had the first one very much in mind. The formerly remote Eastern Orthodox Christians were coming into the ecumenical movement. The two of us, for whom any prospect of Protestant organic union seemed centuries distant, editorially counseled more Protestant resonsiveness to Orthodoxy, even if this meant patient waiting.

"What do you two mean, waiting?"

My colleague tried to buy time. "Dr. Morrison, we thought we were following your own definition of Christian unity. Spell it out again."

So Morrison testily told us that in his view, any group or person in whom the spirit of Christ was somehow manifestly formed has a different kind of claim on other Christians than do those in whom there is no such formation. Then, one of us asked, even if to recognize this in Orthodoxy meant a slowing down of formal reunion processes, did not Dr. Morrison agree that the spirit of Christ was somehow formed in Eastern Christian individuals and groups?

Now his nostrils flared widest. He drew himself erect. But the answer of this tireless nonagenarian spelled out for us how far we were from liberal vision. "Of course, of course," he said. "But if you want to slow down to include Orthodoxy for the day of Christian reunion, *I may not live to see the day!*" Morrison's was a good counterweight to my own more passive or, as we Niebuhrians liked to say, realistic view of change.

How does someone already committed to the parish and historical scholarship get into such a spot of contradiction? In my case, a hobby became a preoccupation. Years in the public libraries had led me to have an addiction to the press. At the seminary a biblical professor once turned back a paper with a middling grade and a comment like this: "Marty, I've been noticing you haunting the magazine room in the library. It seems to me that you read the periodicals scripturally—and the scriptures periodically." Seeking to make a virtue of the necessity to feed my addiction, I

cherished theologian Karl Barth's suggestion that preach-
ers should live between the Bible and the newspapers.

One day near the end of my doctoral work the phone
rang. The voice was that of *Century* editor Harold Fey.
("Fie," he corrected me for the "Fay" I had always read—so
little did I know of the magazine). He had scouted me out.
Would I join the staff? I had to tell him what I told those
college deans about the parish commitment. So we settled
for a moonlighting that still keeps me at the crossroads of
press releases in religion. There I write a weekly column
and many editorials, help decide what articles to publish
and, to a lesser extent, what policies to pursue, review many
books and assign even more for critical notice—a range of
duties that was from the first a strenuous and welcome
counterpart to parish life.

Ever since this moonlighting began I became a subversive
who counsels similar action among others. The minister
who is simply at the disposal of the parish as chauffeur,
mimeographer, ticket-seller, or whatever else, is not likely
to see the emergence of a creative laity and is certain not to
grow in many important ways. Whether it be through
involvement in graduate work, efforts on a zoning or a
hospital board, or participation in counseling programs,
such persons will thus find other outlets for their egos. They
will locate alternative support systems and will no longer
need to turn their congregations into the be-all and end-all
of their emotional flow. Such leaders will be replenished
with fresh ideas and jostled by a different vision, all to the
benefit of the congregation. I have never seen ministers be
inventive when they were the salaried slaves of the
congregation that had them on the payroll. The good ones
always have parallel places for outlet and intake.

At the same time, the best of them develop as a quality
and philosophy of life what Gabriel Marcel calls *disponibilité*,
the ability to "make one's self available" to others. Call it

creative schedule interruption. They are not merely available on trivial levels of the sort that would mean they could never withdraw for study, prayer, enjoyment, or growth. But in the midst of their business they know when to look up and into the depths of human need. While they cultivate their own being, they grow especially responsive to others. But they learn quickly also to resume a life somehow free of the subjects of their care and interaction. They find that, before developing this virtue, all the while they thought they were playing the lackey, they had been playing God.

To mention *disponibilité* is not to claim it. But seven years of weekly commuting at the side of parishioners, with some of whom I lunched downtown on *"Century* day," combined with an ever-expanding schedule of lectures and writing, bred in me a desire to emulate those who demonstrated it. A Swiss compulsion leads me to advertise the fact that after seven years I had missed no Sundays, scheduled meetings, or funerals. There were some crises that did not match the timetable of a compulsive scheduler, but these were few. And what I brought in from the *Century* world helped compensate for them.

That *Century* world was still churchly, and thus it was a buffer between the parish and secular pluralism. In those years its specialty was the ecumenical movement, then at its pre-Vatican II crest. The editors assigned me to cover mainline church conventions. There I learned that liberal churches could be as incivil as traditional bodies, their bureaucracies as unresponsive. But at least they were trying to devise a needed new genre of religious life, one that encouraged commitment at home, combined with under-standing of those at some theological or geographical distance.

On the ecumenical circuit it was clear that membership in an outsider denomination and a role as a reporter for an independent journal would keep my own ecumenical journey at the margins of the movement. But it also freed me to criticize one element of power shift or drift in the leadership. The heirs of those who founded the World Council of Churches, the World Student Christian Federation, and the Federal and later the National Council of Churches, were growing increasingly reflexive and inbred. Their article footnotes cited a canon of authors who were chosen bureaucrats and task force members. The writers simply recycled ideas. To hear the debates at the Faith and Order Commission and the Central Committee of the World Council at St. Andrew's, Scotland, in 1960, was to overhear conversations that often lacked echoes in member denominations, to say nothing of their constituent local churches.

At St. Andrew's there occurred one of those trivial but still revealing serendipities that symbolized trouble for the formal ecumenical movement. The commission was then creatively specifying what was the character of the unity Christians seek. It formulated an excellent phrase to the effect that all in each place who accepted Jesus Christ as Lord and Saviour should come to a "fully committed fellowship." One of the transcribers of these proceedings prepared a press release, which declared that all Christians should come to a "full committee fellowship." That is how the movement had come to appear in the eyes of the congregations.

It has since become fashionable to pile criticisms on the mainline ecumenical movement. Its beneficiaries now take for granted its fruits but rarely acknowledge their roots. I have heard journalist Malcolm Muggeridge tell audiences of Christians that the World Council founders were simply like the drunks outside his town pub—so wobbly that they would fall if they did not sag against one another's drooping shoulders. Yet those founders were not wobblers. They

were people who not long before in two wars had faced one
another across the trenches and in no-man's-land. They
had seen enough futile conflict. Others were people who
broke through old patterns to establish lifesaving postwar
relief missions. Together they had probed scripture and
impelled service. And without them the climate could never
have developed to make possible the very mixed audiences
that were hearing Muggeridge. Their responsive passion
gave rise to the movement, after nine hundred years of
virtually *nothing but* Christian sniping at fellow Christians.
All those years each set of believers had undercut all others,
the faithful crusaded against other faithful, and few
accepted anyone else's ministry. To reverse that trend in
mere decades was astonishing.

Then came the setbacks. What Max Weber called
Rationalität took over. An all-encompassing rational bu-
reaucratic impulse, though it worked among men and
women of general good will, led to administrative self-con-
cern. Unrepresentative leaders often worked for "full
committee fellowship" until the committed home folks
ignored them. The councils also suffered from their
successes. Legatees of their triumphs forgot what the
spiteful earlier Christian world was like. The Second
Vatican Council suddenly blind-sided the Protestant
Orthodox Movement. It created so much drama that the
earlier style of committee work seemed drab by compari-
son. The new Council generated a climate in which on the
local level those who wished to, could constantly share many
practical effects of unity; they became impatient with
prodding the committees.

As a *World* Council, the largest organization after about
1961 tried to do justice to its global constituencies, despite
their conflicting political attachments. Christians from the
Third-World, as it came to be called, spoke up for
anticolonial and neonationalist interests. While their voices

rarely transcended those interests, they did sound like prophets against the idolatries of the northern hemisphere. Some Western leaders then turned passive and readily assented in "yas suh" spirit to every form of ideological criticism from elsewhere. This pattern gave intransigent critics in America a base for propounding elaborate conspiracy theories about the councils, making them bogeys useful in their own schemes.

Not least of all, and most promising, was a trend in which the formerly antiecumenical conservative evangelicals stopped being standoffish. They began to get their own act together, as in the Lausanne Covenant of 1974. As soon as they formed such conferences parallel to those of the World and National Councils, they also began to reach out in dialogue of their own with Roman Catholics and Jews. They did this with evidences of such churchly vitality that these conversations sometimes promised more than did those mainline efforts initiated by Protestant ecumenical forces.

Each generation hears the ecumenical promise. And each one invents a new way to block response. Born to overcome hatreds between church bodies, the Christian unity movement today faces an issue few anticipated. The felt-divisions now never follow denominational lines. Baptists do not attack Methodists who do not attack Catholics. Rarely is a whole large church body any longer a House of Muumbi, which exacts loyalty and teaches suspicions of others. Now the line falls *through* the various houses and tribes. A church is too inclusive to shore up frail identities, so the parties within each church are called into service. The older ecumenical movement was built on a political model. The churches themselves, however, which had once been familial, moved away from their origins, omitted the political mode, and hurried toward a military style. In this pattern, power groups call for unconditional surrender from other sources as soon as they find them at any disadvantage.

Since in the twentieth century the major issues of church life rarely concern God, Christ, or the Holy Spirit, but revolve about personal experience or tribal authority, it is natural that the parties form around these. Pentecostalism or the charismatic movement and reactions to it divide some of the groups. Episcopal-type churches are torn over authority as it relates to what they call tradition. On these terms Marcel Lefebvre threatened schism in Roman Catholicism and the Protestant Episcopal Church in the United States saw some splintering. Most mainline bodies and moderate evangelical groups, on the other hand, were disrupted by parties who wanted to rule out all who did not buy into their particular philosophies about biblical authority. In all cases, both sides professed to adhere to the heart of the constituting faiths of their churches, and they probably did more often than not. But over the new issues aggressive parties found their former brothers and sisters *de trop.* They simply did not wish to share space in the church or under the sun with them. A demonic rage took over, though often the angry had the guise of mere unresponsiveness and only sometimes more the smiles that victorious vandals can afford to affect.

The act of monitoring these conflicts for *The Christian Century* has shown us editors some textbook cases of violent conflict. Any number of theories will explain them. I can stand by with an exposition of Georg Simmel, such as Lewis Coser's *The Functions of Social Conflict,* turn the pages, and watch the warfare confirm the hypotheses therein. Simmel diagnosed the modern disease in which conflict binds groups or, in this case, half-groups, together. Fanatic partisanship helps the insecure maintain boundaries around their hollowed personalities or threatened half-tribes. The conflict need not be realistic. The weapons are

never proportionate to the threat. A deeper human need
drives the antagonist: he or she *must* hate. Such hate is
portable. John Dewey wrote that "men do not shoot because
targets exist, but they set up targets in order that throwing
and shooting may be more effective and significant."

As the conflict progresses, hate intensifies. For Simmel,
"it is *expedient* to hate the adversary with whom one fights,
just as it is expedient to love a person whom one is tied to."
We have seen strange new bedfellowships form in the
half-Houses of Muumbi. Aggression close to home is always
most ugly. If the tribal bonding has been previously
well-defined and especially intimate, the antagonist will
work fiercely to put the other party out. The minority will
appear to produce the renegade who knows the secrets of
the group and who, in Max Scheler's terms, will be tempted
to "engage in a continuous chain of acts of revenge on his
spiritual past."

Once a majority party has learned to relish the effects of
internal conflict, it will turn these also against the outside
world and become ever more sectarian. Thus when the
fundamentalists who formed inerrancy-of-the-Bible parties
split their own churches and drove out opponents, they
went looking for other enemies, thus to hold their cabals
together. Meanwhile, they could tolerate no questions from
within. The dissenter keeps the winners off balance: will he
go to the enemy? Will she set up a rival group? Will he try to
change the tribe? She must be up to something!

The totalist-minded winners have to search constantly
for such enemies. They must be on their guard especially
against any who approach them in a spirit of tolerance or
civility. Let me illustrate. For years, the conservative
evangelical Billy Graham, though he was friendly to it, has
met attack chiefly from the fundamentalist far right. The
"come-outers" on that flank argue that Graham is too
responsive to Christians with whom he has slight disagree-

ments. Instead of being their ally he has to become their main enemy. He then acquires a new name from them like liberal or ecumenical or modernist. In order to make conflict efficient, aggressives have to create a common enemy by imposing unity on varied alternative parties.

Modernism in any case is a better enemy than Billy Graham, since it is important for belligerents to depersonalize conflict, says Simmel. Some years ago Episcopal conversatives did have a heretic on their hands in Bishop James C. Pike, but they bent in many directions not to have to pursue him. They chose instead to psychoanalyze away the threats of "poor old Jim." They were not so restrained when in later battles over Prayer Book revision or the ordination of women they were able to defend the tradition against modernism. Only thus could the struggle look respectable and become sufficiently intense. Persons call forth response, so one must get rid of persons for the sake of issues.

The surprising new denial of the ecumenical promise at home has occurred chiefly in groups that had never previously found motives or means to provide for the expression of hostile feelings. The Democratic Party ordinarily knew better. Day-to-day conflict between its factions let off steam and permitted few accumulated grievances. All was forgotten on General Election Day. Conflict within a church body that had been familial, on the other hand, becomes murderous. Lewis Coser suggests two reasons: first, because the conflict does not deal with a mere immediate issue, but is based on those accumulated grievances. Second, within the confines of the House of Muumbi, the group members are totally involved and they can thus better be mobilized.

When first I was assigned to observe such civil wars in denominations, they seemed relatively unimportant. They do not directly threaten the republic. A New York Jew cares

no more about intratribal warfare in the Southern Baptist
Convention than does a Baptist care about tension in the
Knights of Pythias or the Odd Fellows. A secular-minded
Harvard professor may be nervous over armed Black
Muslim schisms, but she is not likely to duck when
Lutherans are taken over by fundamentalism, as my own
church body was. Mennonites do not feel pain when Marcel
Lefebvre resists Catholic development. Yet, up close,
despite apparent harmlessness, the results can be devastating. If none of them leave in their trail dead bodies and
none demolish the republic, they can destroy lives and
distract energies from the commonweal. As in all obsessive
family battles, they consume the people who are in them.
From a Christian point of view they detract from the unity
and love that are to be marks and tests of the community.

As the malignancy of such conflicts spread we saw
witnesses to the truth turn dispirited. Other people who
knew better assented to great evil. Some came to favor
doctrines or policies that "worked," whether they were true
or not. We have seen faithfulness painted as treason, fidelity
to tradition portrayed as deviance, careers—though not
always vocations—destroyed. We have tried to salvage from
the ruins something positive by trying to discern what it is
that calls forth integrity from those who put career survival
and political expediency second. As Soviet dissident
Vladimir Bulovsky answered when he told why he would
not capitulate to the terror, a person who once arrived at the
notion of inner freedom cannot change it. "It is impossible
as if, as if self-destructive. It's more easy to commit suicide
than to change his beliefs."

Is the ecumenical era over? While I do not bring Charles
Clayton Morrison's liberal optimism to this conclusion, I
would have to say no. The movement is in trouble, but the
spirit is finding new outlets and forms. Our age of
compulsive ingatherings of tribalists is truly fertile. It

constantly sees inventions of new ways to thwart the ecumenical promise. As in the case of so many other forces, while the committed lack civility, the civil often lack conviction. But both, at their best, are in search of different models.

Analysts of diversity-in-unity within the New Testament find patterns of startling variety and conflict already in the church of the first generation. The account in the book of Acts of the first council in Jerusalem shows that the parties then found a political means of dealing with the conflict. There were and are good reasons to protect the diversity. While the danger that a totalist "super church" might now rise internationally is very remote, the hazard that a homogeneous and bland one would emerge once frightened many. The *Century* sent me off to cover an early meeting of the Consultation on Church Unity. It is a well-meant if hundred-years-late attempt to unite mainline Protestant churches. Whether rightly or wrongly, already by then COCU suffered from the perception that its rise would mean that people back home would have to part with the colorings of their cultures, the guts of diverse hymnals, the groundwork of their varied liturgies, and the creative chaos of conflicting policies. Today people are working to find ecumenical patterns that mean an "adding on," not a "smoothing down" of traditions.

Through the decades at the ecumenical watching-post that is *The Christian Century* I have come to see most vitality when people regard the whole Christian church as a sort of "family of apostolic churches," called to demonstrate richer styles of mutual acceptance than we now know. But it must also assure the sense of soils and smells that come with heritages. People are not humans in general or Christians in general. Faith comes as if bonded with certain kinds of organ or guitar tones, the experiences of slave or free peoples, or varied sermonic styles. These are all penultimate, not ultimate matters. But taken together they make up something attractive to people of faith.

Some frustrations do call for immediate attention. If "full committee fellowship" delays, people will either fabricate "fully committed fellowship," or lose heart. Why after so many decades Christians have not been able to move from baptismal to eucharistic fellowship, from shared baptism to shared communion—is there any other kind?—is a puzzle that produces dismay among the biblically responsive. To those who look only to productive achievement in world and church, such a concern is a luxury. But if the core of the person, the congregation, and the church is important, then this moment of ecumenical pause should give pause. What is more central than a free responsory to the free divine invitatory word? As I commuted back to the parish each week from the world of *The Christian Century,* the urgency of the question kept pressing itself. It left no choice for me but to find ways to join those who would help realize greater Christian unity.

. . . Though, of course, I may not live to see the day!

4

Responsiveness: The Civil Demand

After the anesthesia wore off, the victim of an automobile accident woke up in the hospital. As his consciousness returned he took note of tubes running in and out of his body and the support that came with intensive care. He saw the faces of concerned physicians and aides looking down into the slit between bandages that made room for his eyes. Looking past them he saw his bound feet elevated and his bandaged hands, swathed like huge cocoons, pulled ceilingward. At last he was able to gasp out a question, "Doctor, when you take off these bandages, will I be able to play the violin?"

The answer was reassuring. "We have done all that medical science can do. The outlook for your complete recovery is good. Most of all, I can tell you, you *will* be able to play the violin!"

"That's wonderful," said the victim. "I never could before
the accident."

Whenever I hear a story like that I think of an autumn
morning in 1963 when, at the midlife age of thirty-five, as a
true late-starter, I stepped into the classroom to teach.
Leaving the pastoral ministry was accidental. The self-
inflicted damages were emotional, not physical. But for all
the trauma, I might as well have been bandaged.

For years a persistent University of Chicago Divinity
School dean, an assenting faculty, and an endorsing provost
had been inviting me to the faculty as if I were a teacher.
Later I might as well have asked whether or not, when I
recovered from the move that I finally made and the
bandages were off, I would be able to teach. Their answer
would have been, "Of course, . . ." And I would have had to
say, "That's wonderful. I never could before."

After seven years in the mission congregation and eleven
years in parish ministry it was clear that something had to
give. To our own four sons we had added two Mexican-
Americans as "permanent foster children." From time to
time we extended the family with other guests. Such a busy
household made demands on parents that are harder to
meet in the pastorate than in most other vocations. The
parish had grown beyond its original familial size. It needed
a reconceiving that could come only if the founding pastor
moved on.

No dramatic call broke from the heavens into our
mundane world. Signals as usual came through the more
subtle tugs of life. Other people were deciding where my
competence and callings were. A file marked "Vocation"
includes records of eight or nine deanships or presidencies
that were at least half-offered during those years. But
except for a charitable German-speaking parish that once
called me to be its pastor, no other Christian congregation
ever approached. This may be a tribute to the astuteness of

Christian congregations. After one seminary asked me to present its call to our congregational meeting, I learned that members shared the perception that I should be available also for other ministries. While I did not want any kind of administrative post, I now took seriously The University of Chicago teaching offer. This time it came with finality. The Divinity School had to fill the post that was open to me. We could not leave Illinois without leaving behind two (foster) family members. Nowhere else in our state could one teach and probe my subjects so congenially. So, after appropriate wrenchings and tears, we moved.

More dramatic vocational shifts than this go on every day, and I have made too much of this one. Yet the transit bears heavily on the project of this life journey. I had been an administrator of pledges in one House of Muumbi who always felt called to teach responsivenes to the ways of other houses. Now came the opposite problem. The modern academy thinks of itself as a transaction among responsive people, but it makes provision for few caves or shelters where people of a particular faith might gather to call signals.

The modern academy: its religious import unfolds subtly. An interdisciplinary faculty colloquy spelled it out for me one afternoon, when we were attempting to define modernity. I had no tape recording and took no notes. What a sociologist said, therefore, is lost in detail. But, while taking some liberties with phrases, I am sure I have remembered the points of his ten-minute comment:

In the modern world, everything important gets chopped up. It all gets refined, ground up. Instead of being something visible and lumpy it gets thinned out and diffuse. Marty, you and Father X here are walking embodiments of what modernity means in this instance. I know you both well. Off campus I have seen you both in clerical collars. No one says you can't wear them here. If you did, it would be at worst an eccentric affectation. No one would be offended; ministers

and priests are welcome on faculties as much as anyone else—but no
more than anyone else—if they have something to say. It is just that
their badges won't mean privilege, and they probably won't ever find
any reason to wear badges. I know you both say Mass on Sundays and
you are part of congregations. But that just isn't a relevant part of
your or anyone else's biography on the campus. Religion is a private
affair. It is invisible.

That paraphrase is close to the gist of some works on
sociology of religion; Thomas Luckmann's *The Invisible
Religion* is the most appropriate of them. The issue for
religious and all other kinds of tribes in modernity, be they
racial, ethnic, cultural, or ideological, is the way they are
chopped up into almost pure individualisms. Their
adherents tend to become Robinson Crusoes of faith,
temporarily disrupted from community and place, who live
in semicongenial "islands." Such circumstances have a
bearing on manners. If people are to coexist, there must be
civility, even if at the cost of conviction.

The tribal side in many ways remained somewhat more
vivid for me than it would for many people to whom
religion is important. Perhaps some Orthodox Jews,
Eastern or Roman Catholic Christians, or oriental religionists would have borne more visible badges. Fundamentalists
of any faith would come with more potent reinforcements.
But I did bring credentials—for which, of course, no one
ever asked—from my church body. Through some act of
vision "it seemed good to them and the Holy Spirit" to get
two men, Joseph Sittler and Arthur Carl Piepkorn, to help
draft a Diploma of Vocation. So I retain a welcome if
somewhat anomalous call to be a secular university
professor. This call formally elicits a special kind of mutual
responsibility in respect to the church but without limiting
my freedom in the university.

The tendency of church bodies to circumscribe ministerial vocations and define calls ever more parochially in

recent years, while it is bureaucratically neat, seems to me a thoughtless move. People like me are glad to carry "the burden of ordination" into the pluralist classroom setting. Implicit criticisms of the church that then come through in my historical inquiries have a different ring, at least to the speaker, than were I a wholly mobile potshotter from without. Yet it must also be said that such a very slight mark of visibility is a barely discernible badge. It does not represent the only way to carry on our kind of work. The call includes no perquisites and is not likely to be noticed in workaday university life. It thus helps spell out part of what modernity means.

While the processes of modernity chop up religion, diffuse it, push it to the margins, and leave it a subject of choice, religion as such does belong in the university world. The journey from parish to university did not mean leaving religion behind on secular soil. In any accounting of "how my mind has changed since," I would cite a transit from thinking chiefly about the meaning of "the secular" to the implications instead of "the modern." Prepared long before to see the university and its world as the victim and agent of secularism, of studied godlessness, I have come to see them more and more as catalysts instead for modernity.

A graphic metaphor often comes to mind to illustrate this. Religion was not a kind of substance like air in a leaking balloon. Instead it represented a dimension of human life comparable to the substance in an unleaking balloon. But a hand with spread fingers regularly presses on it. This pressure causes the balloon to take different shapes at different times. It becomes protean; every shape can become another shape. The effect of such shifting does not make life for people of convictions easier, but that life is different than the prophets of pure secularism envisioned that it would be.

This picture has developed in frequent intellectual

encounters, but some of them made it especially vivid. Participating in consultative conferences for a papal commission provided clarity of outline. Both at the Second Vatican Council and offstage, Pope John XXIII used to speak of moderns as if they formed concentric circles around the Roman Catholic Church. Beyond the Orthodox-Protestant "separated brothers and sisters" came the Jewish cousins. In their trail were the Islamic shirttail relatives, followed by the people of other faiths who could express the virtues of the search for God. But beyond all of these people were those of good will who did not know God. Traditionalists and other curious people kept asking who these folks were. Among whom or through whose good will did God work, even when the people did not know it or did not recognize God? Pope Paul VI set out to address this question with a commission *non credendi*, or "nonbelievers." Now the church could tackle secularism head on.

Cardinal Franziskus Koenig of Vienna, in subsequent conferences at Rome and near Vienna, convoked scholars who might help locate the *non credendi*. Of course, the Cardinal, a sophisticated observer, needed only to look out his window to see atheists, agnostics, and ignorers passing by. Secularity can fall like an oppressive mist on post-Christian European cities or can come like a sunburst of freedom into its gloomier corners. But this secularity turns out to be elusive to analysts. It, too, is subject to the diffusion of modernity. Like religion, it is everywhere and nowhere. Theologians might be tempted to make normative judgments about the quality of faith and nonfaith. But most of us consultants were not systematic theologians but social scientists who turned up little nonbelief in organized social forms.

Instead we kept finding other-belief and, often, over-belief. Sometimes these took the form of forces that wanted to overcome modernity. That is, they wanted to counter chopped-upedness and choice in religion. These included Nazism, Communism, and Maoism. Such movements tried to force people into huge and efficient new Houses of Muumbi coextensive with the nation itself. They were messianic after historic faiths had lost their similar trust. They had a finer sense of heresy and a stronger impulse to excommunicate than did most old inquisitors in the churches. They came rich with dogma and scripture, myth and symbol, ritual and social forms, philosophical meanings and behavioral prescriptions. Whatever else they were, they were not made up of *non credendi*.

While leaders coerced people to comply with these monopolistic political religions, there were also more genteel aspirations. Among these were some forms of the American religion, a largely voluntary common national faith that allowed people to practice their private cults alongside it. More potent in the minds of their adherents were historic religions that were now tied to political movements. Almost all of them were resurgent fundamentalisms of the kind that has since regained political power in Shi'ite Islamic Iran. Not yet so well known were Jewish hard-line impulses like the Gush Emunim movement that uses the ancient Bible to assert its claims on the West Bank in Israel. Older and slightly milder than the Gush Emunim was *Opus Dei,* a militant force in Catholic Spain. Belligerent Protestants in America were to promote Christian Embassies, Christian Yellow Pages, or a lobby called Christian Voice to stake out their exclusivisms. Wherever we sought *non credendi* we found uprooted young people looking for identity and authority in new cults, substitutes for their families. Nor did we lack the sight of sects, whose members foraged for recruits more effectively than did belongers to more civil-minded churches. Beyond them all were millions of "invisible religionists," people without badges or visible group support. These private enterprisers and consumers of religions prospered in and around universities and industrial cities.

Cynics consider many of these movements to be religious only epiphenomenally. That would mean that religion was only extra baggage attached to forces that could exist apart from them and that analysts could explain in nonreligious terms. Take the matter of warfare. Since the Second World War most civil and international killing has had a dimension that Harold Isaacs calls racial-ethnic-tribal-religious. Secular-minded observers take the first three parts of that link seriously, but see religion itself as an accidental tagalong. They reduce the conflict and find it to be "nothing but," say, economic.

In their terms, the Shi'ite and Shahist parties in Iran were fighting over "nothing but" the tyranny of the Shah, and not over what modernity was doing to tribal religion. Hindu and Muslim forces were contending only for their parts of the economic pie and subcontinental land in Asia. Bangladesh and Pakistan were creations of merely political movements. In their eyes, Arabs and Israelis fought for turf, and millennial-old scriptures or traditions were used only to justify their outrages. To the "nothing but" people, African tribalists fought for the hell of it, or to enlarge boundaries, but never because the spirit of Muumbi called them to it. In this vision, there are never holy wars or jihads. The efforts by humans to respond to unseen powers are, to the "nothing buttery" observers, simply covers-up for other things that must *really* matter in a secularized world.

The Roman papers found it useful to describe the *non credendi* conferences as having to deal *de ateismo,* concerning atheism. The main point of the findings, that the world was full of very old and very new, sometimes promising and often ominous, rarely civil and occasionally murderous beliefs—these were observed by headlines about nonbelief or opposition to religion.

Many in the American academy and the mass media have even more difficulty than did Roman newspapers grasping the power of new religiosities and old. The nation itself is so pluralistic that its many contending forces tend to cancel one another out; they make one another seem trivial. The election of a born-again president and of Pope John Paul II helped rescue religion from the obituary pages of the Saturday newspapers and bring it to prime time and page one. So did some stories of cults, like the one that ended in suicide at Jonestown or others that cause parents to pay deprogrammers to kidnap their children. You could lose the entire membership of many of these cults in the youth rooms of huge First Baptist Church in Dallas. But the exotic groups recruited among the children and students of university professors. This feature made their religious *Putsches* more newsworthy than were the weekly lives of much larger but more conventional-looking churches.

What should academicians make of the fact that nine out of ten Americans find it important to tell polltakers that they believe in God? If that response might come with the jerk of a knee, another is less reflexive: eight out of ten keep wanting to amend the United States Constitution in order to establish prayer in public schools. Are people *non credendi* when, in an age in which organized religion is easily escapable, six out of ten citizens find reasons to adhere to it, and two-thirds of these claim to have attended worship within the week? This is an age when neither the threat of the civil sword nor hell itself keeps them there. Such attendance is far higher than it was in the ages of faith in the Western world, in times like the Middle Ages or colonial America. Many may attend out of habit, but the value of participating for the sake of social status or to be conformist is weaker every year. Are the believers searching for lost fathers? Are they out to replace waning illusions with new ones? Humans act for reasons too complex for anyone to reduce. But the sense that people should respond to unseen powers that act upon them spurs them to a search for meaning and belonging. The search assures that scholars in the field of religion are not likely to run out of subject matter soon.

Religion, as our colleague put it, was "everywhere but nowhere" until we began looking for *non credendi* through the eyes of papal commissions or the American university. It is even more invisible in another zone to which the professorial calling took me. On many occasions I have found myself the only, or almost the only, scholar from what news magazines call "the world of religion" on humanist panels. These included the founding board of the National Humanities Center, the Commission on the Humanities, a state Humanities Council, consultative task forces for the American Academy of Arts and Sciences, and the like. This gravitational pull toward anything with the word *humanities* in it has, by the way, forced me to rethink the meanings of a Christian humanism. The portrait of the civil Christian scholar Erasmus belongs on my office wall next to that of passionately tribal Martin Luther.

Humanists define the Humanities as including history, philosophy, literature, linguistics, *and* religion. On these panels the historians have plenty of company; the philosophers gather in groups; but the religious scholar could hold his or her caucus in a phone booth. Religion seems to sneak in by osmosis, capillary action, hitchhiking, acting the barnacle, or as afterthought. Even in my own case, membership in the historical profession apart from religion is often a sufficient credential. Religion in the humanities wears no badges and has no privileges. In fact, when public funding is visible, religion is especially invisible, lest watchdog taxpayers get the idea that study of religion is support for religion. Little do they know that to some visceral creedalists the study of religion is regarded as subversive of religion!

In earlier ages my participation on humanist soil would have looked like a foray *in partibus infidelium,* in the territories of the infidel. Yet it is invisibility of religion, not infidelity, that prevents many scholars from accurately assessing power in the world today. When it becomes visible, people who never thought they cared rise from apathy. Some civil scholars engage in arguments whose positions they ground in childhood faiths that have become victims of arrested growth syndromes. Other debaters display sophisticated but previously submerged understandings of religion. Still others, over coffee or at the airport, let traces of their own badges show. They must hurry home for Sabbath sundown, or to sing in the Christmas oratorio at the Episcopal church. I have heard a planning group dismiss the subject of "Superstition Among Academics" as a legitimate topic for inquiry because it does not exist. And then, later at cocktails, we learned that some members were absent because their spouses would not let them fly that week. There had been two jet crashes and, "after all, they always come in threes—and this *is* Friday the thirteenth."

At times it seems as if the world is too neatly divided in two. On the one hand are those civil but uncommitted academic people, elites who pore over books or sip Manhattans. On the other hand are those convinced but uncivil tribalists who cut one another up in Iran, Israel, India, Ireland, and Iowa. Does the line of Yeats' poem "The Second Coming," "The best lack all conviction and the worst are full of passionate intensity," apply? No. Best and worsts are hard to measure here. And the lines are not so clear. Many empathic but firm believers use religion to bind and to heal, to promote concord and not war. And many serene collegians and their mentors are fair game for bizarre cults that street-wise ghetto youth would resist any day because they know a hustle when they see one. Or they turn the academy itself into a belligerent tribe.

The modern university bulletin board symbolizes the blurring of old lines. Tucked between and sometimes over notices about courses in science and opportunities in business are melanges of appeals for students to join Hillel and Newman Foundation and Campus Crusade. From there on over the board is a supermarket for most of the religions, systems of magic, or superstitions ever known. It beckons to a world of intimacy without commitment, and parades subjects one is advised to be "into"—Zen, Jesus, tarot cards, the cabala, the Latin Mass, the Holy Spirit, witchcraft—until a new celebrity or roommate invites one to be "into" another new clientele. Modernity breeds a hunger for wholeness in the most unlikely outposts and backwaters, including the university itself.

The phrase "hunger for wholeness" captures much. We are told that the Jew feels chopped up ever since modernity severed ethnicity from religion. The Catholic is still adjusting to the sundering of church from state. Protestants feel cut off from congenial soil in protected regions. The trip from the *Southern* Baptist Convention to pluralist Washington, D.C., is one that calls even the chief executive to leave badges behind or to forego many visible privileges. Profound commitments get to be sequestered in the private sphere of family life, leisure, or holy days. In a balkanized America, the old mainstream WASP culture no longer sets forth the norms for society. People do not know against what to rebel or with whom to conform. Skeptical academics often keep this hunger for wholeness in check. Their students and children find it more difficult to ignore. Some become as if religiously obsessed with their careers or various hedonisms. Others sample the smorgasbord of half-faiths. And not a few in recent years have been satisfying their hunger by sitting at table under authoritarian father figures who propound very uncivil ideologies.

I joined the academy just in time to see two great tribal movements threaten civility. They came and went as but two waves in a motion that is likely to produce others in years to come. Together they made up most of what professors mean when they rue "the late sixties." One was called the counterculture, a movement of flower children who professed to be gentle. Yet, as Theodore Roszak, their chronicler, pointed out, they came on as new barbarians who trained their eyes of fire and verbal weaponry on traditions of humane learning. They wanted to reject legacies which they felt they no longer possessed, but which possessed them.

The people of the counterculture were the victims of modernity, afflicted with wholeness-hunger. They wanted to take nature whole and reject technology out of hand. To that end they hopped jet aircraft toward Woodstock festivals, where they listened to electronically amplified guitars. Presumably they cherished anesthesia and high-speed drills when a tooth ached. To their credit, they did stimulate a sense of wonder, and may have inspired some to take a second look at their natural environment. But when rebelled-against parents withdrew fiscal support or when it became necessary to line up at the job trough, many ran for cover and turned straight.

Just in time. A movement born to stimulate empathy had turned out to be tribalist. It had no room for old people, blacks, the poor, deviants from its own norms, straights, parents, professors, or people who worked for a living. Even the Jewish and Christian versions of this counterculture, which momentarily produced the Children of God and the Jesus People, turned out to be hard-line huddlers in their own House of Muumbi, not genteel at all.

The other case study was less overtly religious, though

many of its adherents treated their ideology with a
fanaticism that would have made the crusaders and
inquisitors envious. My own contacts with the counterculture had occurred on travels or in the classroom. The
climate of and around The University of Chicago was too
gray and grim for it, not as congenial as the environs of
Benares-on-the-Charles, Boulder, or Berkeley. But the
second assault, in the form of campus militancy, came very
close to home. The militant protest of the late sixties rose
from plausible sources: shock over unjust racial situations,
the disparity between poor and rich, the lack of power
among the oppressed, and the misuse of power in the
Vietnamese War. Like other such movements, this one
attracted people of many sorts, from conscientious critics
and utopians to people given over to Oedipal rage or a
Manichaeism that simplified the world into Bad God and
Good God, Bad Guy and Good Guy forces.

Some militants were merely practical; they protested,
"Hell, no, we won't go!" to the military draft. Others
developed into justifiable but eventually irrational forms of
dissent, which led in the end to the burning of black or
Hispanic ghettos. Most ideological was the storming of the
civil academy by its own young, often members of the upper
middle class. Reformers could work for political redress
after a ghetto uprising. But nihilist utopians who wanted to
bring down the military-industrial complex by locking up a
dean, burning the files of a humane researcher, or bombing
a mathematics building with a mathematician inside, came
with nonnegotiable demands.

The council of the Senate of The University of Chicago is
a fifty-one person body of faculty members elected at large.
It provided my vantage for observing how fragile is the
veneer of civility over the modern academy. During a
takeover of the Administration Building, for who knows or
who ever knew what purpose, we met regularly at venues

that had to be changed in the light of recurring threats of physical danger. Veterans of the council from those years still tend to speak in a sense of communion when they recall their beleaguerment. We took comfort in knowing that many of the people who were vandalizing the building and trying to shut down the campus were not our own students, and then lost comfort to think that they were, however, someone's students or dropouts from somewhere. They were not blue-collar workers, deprived blacks, or the rural poor.

The metropolitan press taunted the university president for not "calling in the cops" to put down the barbarians. In Chicago, a few months after the 1968 Democratic Convention, the men in blue represented the messiah to the holders of the Administration Building. A disruption of two hundred would have turned into an eruption of two thousand had they appeared. Almost daily the president, whose courage rubbed off on our highly diverse council, asked whether he should satisfy the demand for instant law and order, and each time he won unanimous support not to. The threat finally passed. It is quite likely that his stand represented a turn from the anticivil style that almost overwhelmed the universities and helped return the day in which conflict included debate over negotiable issues.

We had all been trained to look for assaults on the academy from the right in the McCarthy era in the fifties. But in the sixties, the vandals came from the far left. The 180-degree turn in the source taught the academy never to overlook any direction when monitoring or surveying potential assaults. Such a vision could lead to paranoia, but the academy ought to have sufficient internal variety and enough resilience not to overreact. In the aftermath, however, one thought ought to keep on embarrassing the academy. How could its products, university students, be so ignorant about the climate of America, which was not then in a pre-Revolutionary circumstance? How could they be so uninformed about the anatomy of revolution as to act as they did?

One of the nonnegotiable demands that reached us was that a certain proportion of incoming freshman classes be made up of sons and daughters of blue-collar workers, in order to assure a proletariat. We would have been reaching into the most anti-revolutionary cohort in America, the people most likely to want to keep things as they were. Some of the rebel outcry and outrage may have helped make possible valid reforms by other controversial but less violent contenders like Martin Luther King, Jr., Dorothy Day, or Cesar Chavez, but they also provided opponents of these causes with banners and bogeys. See, it was said, this is what *all* protests look like. It was hard then for the public to take seriously the protests of people whose previous way of life did buy them the credentials to propose alternative patterns.

With a measure of pride I count only six paragraphs devoted to the subject of barbarianism in the citadels of civility. But alert readers have reasons to be suspicious: these words may obscure from view other sources of unresponsiveness in the academy. In the language of the late Herbert Marcuse, the campus was supposedly a source of "repressive tolerance." That is, the university was interlocked with a system whose parts meshed so well that none could escape it. Yes, it was true, the campus defended dialogue, argument, controversy, and the free pursuit of learning. All this in the name of tolerance. Yet as a whole it was the tool of military-industrial complexes or exploitative capitalism, systems that knew they must tolerate and could then buy off discontent or stifle dissent.

Such charges came with just enough ideological thud to make them hard to use for finding analytic tools. But they also arrived with just enough appropriateness that one must still take them seriously while dissecting the academy after the attacks. A saying of the late character Pogo, tacked on my study door, applies to the academy as much as to the church, "We have faults we haven't even used yet." Dependent as it must be upon tax funds or private support, the higher academy will never be so free as its advocates might like to picture it. In economic hard times the university may be more tempted than before to limit the scope of its inquiry and criticism behind the façade of academic freedom and openness. Yet the theme of repressive tolerance as an all-purpose attack obscures the internal resources that come with diversity in the university. It also may lead the attackers to overlook the repressive *in*tolerance that has come with the kinds of socialist regimes that the Marcuseans of a decade before touted as replacements to the present system.

More important than such ideological devices for calling the university into question is the need for alertness to more subtle kinds of unresponsiveness in the purportedly civil academy. Father John Courtney Murray rightfully claimed that the barbarian in our society would not wear bearskins or carry a club. He would be clad in a Brooks Brothers suit or academic tweeds. She would as likely be disguised in an academic robe and come wielding a ballpoint pen. Murray spoke back in the fifties when Protestants, Jews, and Catholics were still trying to read one another out of legitimacy in the republic. But more emphatically he pointed to the way the secular ethos had turned into secular*ism* of a very prejudicial sort.

Murray claimed that when truly troubling or creative issues came up in the republic, citizens had to "go up higher," beyond banal chatter and mere pragmatism, into the realms of ethics, metaphysics, or theology. But the modern academy, he thought, barbarously rules them out. Sometimes it does so claiming that separation of church and state forbids their discussion. At other times, guardians of university freedom remember how hard it was for the academy to transcend its sectarian origins in order to incorporate pluralism. It does not want to revert to its older style.

Twenty years after Murray we can see the results of this handicap in a troubling issue like legal abortion. What is called an abortion debate is really an uncivil war between bearers of bumperstickers. These divide the world in two camps misnamed Pro-Life and Pro-Choice. Each parades its premises as conclusions: Abortion Is Murder, or A Woman's Body Is Hers to Do with What She Wants. Many of the antiabortion forces have shown themselves to be barbarian, not simply in tactic—demonstrators on most causes have been less than genteel—but in their argument. When they insist on sending to legislatures otherwise incompetent people whose only qualification is support for antiabortion measures, they show a loss of interest in the *res publica,* the commonweal of the republic.

Barbarianism on the other side is less visible in the academy. It takes the form of the argument that to oppose abortion is simply an attempt to impose the teachings of a particular church body on the republic. This line of thought shows how atrophied is the ability to "go up higher" into ethics, metaphysics, or theology. The antiabortion people, behind their billboards and in spite of their scuffling strategies, raised profound and legitimate issues. These were not only partly scientific—when does life begin?—but also philosophical and theological. The fetus has rights. The fetus alone does not have all the rights. So far both sides tend to agree. To move beyond this agreement takes one into metaphysics of a sort that no dogmatic church body monopolizes. I have heard Chicago-trained Aristotelian atheists make conscience-stinging "theological" attacks on casual abortion. The Pro-Life people may not hear them because they seek to overpower, not to persuade. But when the civil academician does not listen either, one must note a barbarian heart under the tweeds, a tribal mind under the mortarboard.

To take this stance puts one into some unlovely company. Let me remain scandalous, citing one issue that is unattractive to me and then, at greater length, a more compelling one. First, the Kanawha County, West Virginia, fundamentalists—who have since picked up company from Texas to California—have *half* a point when they urge that biblical "creationism" be discussed alongside evolution in public schools. The academy sneers at such Baptist tribalism. But the sectarians lose their point when they go on to demand that creationism be taught as the truth about life. There is no way one could come to entertain its theories apart from belief in a particular scripture of a peculiar religious group. In no other way would it occur to anyone to believe that the universe came into being in six days. On constitutional grounds the proponents are out of order in their claim. But they effectively do show how observations about evolution and its theory have acquired a creedal status among others. They do generate an ethos and an ethic, a metaphysic and a theology. Without much examination they have gained privileged status. Academic skeptics, not half-lettered fundamentalists, should have pointed this out long ago.

More to the point is the way American civil religion, though itself a sect among the sects, has for two hundred years had a privileged position. This faith derives from the era of the Enlightenment. Civil religion can, it is true, be an ethos without any content. Historian Daniel J. Boorstin argued that the American shrine was as empty as was the Jewish Holy of Holies, which the soldiers of Pompey crashed. But Sidney E. Mead, who called civic faith "the religion of the republic" and Robert N. Bellah, who looked to it for transcendent justice, were among the many who did find substance along with aura in this religion. For Mead, this faith kept alive the Enlightened founders' belief that there was a Supreme Being, that citizens had a duty to be moral, that rewards and punishments must accompany moral or immoral action, and that the republic must promote such transsectarian values at the expense of the irrelevant sects. To Mead the sects were heretical, schismatic, and un-American, in the light of republican faith, though Bellah looked to churches with some hope.

At the moment the American civic faith is in eclipse. Citizens came to care too little about anything beyond private morale to have regard for the republic. Words like *Vietnam* and *Watergate* symbolized a loss of moral credibility and American mission abroad and at home. Subcommunities in America, be they based on race, gender, class, generation, creed, or caucus, do more than the nation to provide citizens with identity and power. It may be that some of us who once threw rocks through the stained glass in the American shrine—as I did in *The New Shape of American Religion* in 1959—may have to help repair it in a time when national community is so hard to regain. As a member of numerous subcommunities, I think this can be done better with Benjamin Franklin's model of public religion than Rousseau's civil religion. Franklin wanted these existing subcommunities and sects to promote the commonweal at the point of their intersections and overlappages. In the European Enlightenment pattern the faith of the state was a straight-out competitor to the other sources of social morale. But to the degree that such a public religion recovers, academicians have to be watchful about its privileged and preemptive status.

Advocates of tuition tax credits for use in supporting private and parochial schools have seen this problem better than have many scholars in the universities. While the public faith is broadly acceptable to majorities, dissenters from it have successfully shown that it *is* a particular creed as well. The Amish, the Jehovah's Witnesses, and sometimes even some Catholics and Calvinists have made this fact stand out in bold relief. No philosophy department today formally propagates the notion that the Enlightenment outlook is the truth about life. Few contend that its Supreme Being is empirically verifiable. As much as I admire Thomas Jefferson, the best articulator of republican creeds, I must know that he was sectarian about his own. From Jefferson to John Dewey in *A Common Faith* there runs the plea that Americans should regard the civil faith or social religion as the very truth about existence, that they make their creed explicit and militant, and that they use it to counter the faiths of the sects.

In two decisions in the 1960s the United States Supreme Court recognized how sectarian the established civil religion was. Both had to do with conscientious objection to military service. The second and more radical decision allowed for the formation of conscience through the study of history or social science, and not exclusively through religion. More devastating to the substance of the religion of the republic was the first judgment, a recognition that not all religions did include faith in anything like a Supreme Being. This meant that logically and legally, conscientious objectors could be religious without such a faith, even though it was integral to the thought of the founders and has been in the canon in American public institutions. When supporters of tuition tax credits point out that they are being taxed to uphold a faith in which they do not believe and one that partly contradicts their own, it is a temptation in the higher academy to be positively uncivil about their claims. The opponents are not anti-Catholic in an atavistic sense, as some defensive Catholics have claimed. They are simply not ready to be what academic people are asked to be: debaters and not dogmatists, people who examine their own assumptions, who are ready to realize that they are not so value-free as they suggest.

These paragraphs make use of what Paul Tillich called the Protestant principle of inquiry and protest against the university. There is another side to academic life. The academy is a congenial base for these stages of my life journey. With Dietrich Bonhoeffer, I have to confess that very often it is easier to find a kind of spiritual communion with many of its profound agnostics than with one party of the ruthlessly pious in the church. Fellow-believers have displayed sustained barbarian hatreds of a sort that one is not likely to see in the pluralist university.

While they may wear no badges and claim no privileges, intense believers do have good reasons to encounter the university at its skeptical best. Believing as I do that doubt is the fuel on which faith feeds and that challenge is the agent that keeps it vivid, I have often listened to hear students say that they did not know what faith was until they tested it in the university. They were unsure of their values until these met critical attacks by people who shared few of them. This is one reason that we have found it valuable to make use of Paul Ricoeur's concept of a "second naiveté." One first looks out critically at the world as the child in the tribe, where walls confine and ceilings are low. After passing through the critical stage, one can suspend disbelief and, the second time, believe *through* interpretation. Within the university and other pluralist centers, people can grow in fidelity to their own tradition. They do not have to become ex-Catholics, ex-Jews, or ex-Baptists in order to become respectable. The world of ex-faiths often propels them to the consumerist religions or leaves them in the blur of modernity, deprived of the measure of shelter that whole persons often should welcome.

I have seen this traditioning process occur also outside

the Divinity School in the other faculties where I teach, the History Department, the Committee on the History of Culture, and the Undergraduate College. There pluralism is most intense; my tribal badges are invisible and offer no advantage. Yet the subject comes up constantly. One sees it in the ways younger siblings of the counterculturalists and militants find their way back to the grandparental world, if not yet to that of their parents. I will paraphrase a typical essay by a student who was fulfilling a college assignment to trace what his people had been doing since they got off the boat, and how he felt about the tradition.

My grandfather was a rabbi in a *shtetl* before Hitler came. After he got in trouble with a woman he migrated to California and tended grapes. Eventually he married a Catholic woman. They were both uprooted and compromised by practicing neither of their traditions. This meant that my father grew up never knowing who he was or what he believed. When he was young, my grandfather had a certain kind of power with a couple of hundred people. At the *Shul* people felt close to him. He knew and taught the Book. When the candle burned low, people would consult him. He could always say the prayer. That was one kind of power. My father is a lawyer in the Loop. Every day he represents cases that involve millions. That's power. In the evening he comes home to the suburbs. He still has no idea who he is. It takes him two-thirds of a bottle of Scotch each night to fill the void and make him forget what he does not really remember. I want grandfather's kind of power.

Such essays are as romantic as they are revealing. Modernity occasions such searches and the university allows for them, so long as it is open, inquiring, a place for argument. But its constituents can never relax. No one in 1960 foresaw the forces that threatened its civility in the decade that followed. Is it safe in the 1980s? And is it ready in its diminished and defensive state to be responsive to the civil demands of a new decade?

What demands?

Those who might here expect a call to follow up on Father John Courtney Murray's attack on interfaith barbarianism will be disappointed. These are not the days to mount a crusade in support of such tolerance. At least on the most broad and superficial level, tolerance never had it so good. The Gallup Poll in 1979 found only negligible hostility in the historic Protestant-Catholic-Jewish triad. Soon more than 100 percent of the people, it would seem, are likely to be tolerant. Only 2 percent of the Protestants could think of any unpleasant experiences that might inspire any dislike of Catholics—down from 9 percent in the Holy War Era of 1952. Only 2 percent of all Christians had similar encounters with Jews and only 1 percent of the Catholics found reasons for a grudge against Protestants. Only 11 percent of the Protestants thought Catholics were grasping for too much power, down from a more ominous 41 percent in 1952. Only 6 percent of the Catholics worried about Protestant power. Whatever happened to the terrible majority? Only 12 percent of the Christians worried about Jewish power. We can all go to sleep. Gallup credits the growth of tolerance to the tripling of the college-trained population since 1935. Congratulations to the academy.

The portentous issue is not a problem of too much *in*tolerance but the loss of faith in tolerance or civility or in the attitudes those two blighted terms once represented. New generations have forgotten the hard-won battles for academic and religious freedom. The voice of Soviet dissidents speaks from a different world. Few notice how difficult it is to assure the constitutional rights of minorities. They seem unaware of how precarious all ententes in intergroup fields are. When cults come along, the first temptation is to revoke their civil liberties—a sure sign that the veneer of assurance is very thin.

Tolerance deserves something of its bad name. Once it meant that an established or host culture owed it to dissent

or guest cultures to let them exist. From there tolerance
degenerated to mean, as G. K. Chesterton said, the virtue of
people who did not believe anything. Father Robert J.
Gannon found it the lowest form of human cooperation,
the drab, uncomfortable, halfway house between hate and
charity. The secular world thought little more of it.
Bertrand Russell twitted the camp of believers by claiming
that toleration rose when people found religion to be less
important than before. Arnold Lunn called mutual
toleration the product of doubt, not of faith. Will Durant
found tolerance growing only where faith lost certainty;
"certainty is murderous." A time has come in which some
people are so sick of uncertainty that a bit of murderousness
looks attractive again.

A far more valuable concept is the one I have often used
here: civility. It takes root from citizens' concern for the
civitas, the human city. In order to coexist and interact, they
had to adopt a mode which originally meant that they would
not behave in a barbarian or anticivil way. Only recently has
civility come to be posed over against commitment or
conviction and seen as the tool of dominant classes in
cultures to rule others out. In books that vary in tone from
puckish to profound, John Murray Cuddihy has described
The Ordeal of Civility and promoted resistance to its manners
in *No Offense*. His is a cry from the heart, a chronicle of
modern hungerings for wholeness. Cuddihy wonders what
happens to people when they only "happen to be Jews."
What is left when religion becomes a private affair and
Catholics no longer must believe that outside their church
there is no salvation? What comes of Protestant certainty
when it stops being murderous and calls off its mission to
bring an end to Judaism through conversion? Where does
one gain the sense of wholeness that came in the close
illusions created by the tribe? What is left of a faith for
which martyrs die in an age of Christian humanism? What

kind of faith is it that is ready to be packed away with collars on Sunday noon, after which its badges disappear and its dogmas blur? Why make anything of old diplomas of vocation if one cannot use them to offend Jews and scandalize agnostics?

No wonder, in the face of plausible answers to such questions, that my *Oxford English Dictionary* says that the word *civil*, "the state of being civilized: freedom from barbarity," is "sinking" in recent usage, to "decently polite." What is left of the passion that produced saints and missionaries, in the decent politeness of interfaith teacupping? Yes, the world is becoming more crowded and better armed. Yes, its tribes are turning terrorist. But is not the civil style too high a price to pay for the alternatives to tribalist militancy?

Rather suddenly, in response to valid questions like those, it has become fashionable to speak in tones of nostalgia for intolerance and incivility in religion. The new anticivilists grow nostalgic for the crusading spirit. They can see in their minds' eyes the sun glinting off silver spears and highlighting white horses. They hear the crusaders' hymns and follow their red crosses. And the taunting academic nonbeliever implies that only crusading faith carries conviction, it alone is real faith. Forgotten is the bridle-rein-deep blood in which crusaders rode over piles of heads, hands, and feet in Jerusalem. Overlooked, too, is the cramping concept of God implied in crusades. Raymond of Agiles from on the scene, remembered: "Indeed, it was a just and splendid judgment of God, that this place should be filled with the blood of the unbelievers when it had suffered so long from their blasphemies." But instead of encouraging a different mode of looking at God, a better means of sustaining conviction, many otherwise gentle folk of secular outlook choose to be condescending about faith that does not call for blood.

At many gatherings of humanists one will hear a twitting of all nonmurderous faiths as being uncertain. The teasers may see the truth in Mr. Dooley's claim that a fanatic is a man that "does what he thinks th' Lord wud do if he knew the facts in th' case," but they do not measure the dangers in such fanaticism. As for Pro-Life or other fanatics—be they pro- or antihomosexual rights, pro- or anti-ERA—at least we hear, you have to admire them for believing *something* deeply. You have to give those pesty Jehovah's Witnesses credit for *true* faith! Such admiration does not often go as deep as C. G. Jung's probing. He thought fanaticism may be "overcompensated doubt." You will hear instead: so Marcel Lefebvre wreaks holy havoc in Catholicism? You have to hand it to him, he knows what *real* Catholicism is, which is more than the popes John and Paul and John Paul and John Paul ever did. Maybe World War III will start because of Gush Emunim fundamentalism or its Islamic counterparts in Iran. As the nuclear clouds of the superpowers form, the anticivilists will have the last satisfaction of boasting that they knew what the real heart of faith looked like. That is more than the diplomats and modernizers knew.

On a far more harmless scale the mistrust of civility in American religious life increased in the 1970s. Because so many civil believers showed so little conviction, some made it a law of history that one could not be civil by convincement. In *Why Conservative Churches Are Growing* Dean M. Kelley properly showed how the loss of tribe and tradition did not serve people well. But tacticians made less proper use of his observation that sects given over to absolutism, fanaticism, zeal, authoritarianism, and unquestioned discipline tended to prosper. The mean-minded groups used his analysis to legitimate their belligerence. Almost humorous, however, were efforts by some formerly

civil people to "play catch-up ball" by deciding to be just a
little bit absolutist, fanatic, zealous, authoritarian, or
demanding of conformity. Fortunately for the republic,
they did not become very good at their efforts. Unfortuna-
tely for the same republic, they did begin to lose faith in the
need to be civil.

What should have given the game away was Dean M.
Kelley's very useful grading of churches from least-ecu-
menical to most-ecumenical. He was able to show that the
standoffish groups prospered in their belligerence while
the open-minded ones lost their boundaries and their cores,
gave people few reasons to join them, and languished. The
successful aggressives were, among others, Black Muslims,
Jehovah's Witnesses, Orthodox Jews, Churches of Christ,
Latter-Day Saints, Seventh-Day Adventists, and the like. No
set of American churches held tenets differing more
radically from one another's than these, a sure sign that
conservative could not equal true. But even those moder-
ates who lost faith in intrinsic views of truth and turned
instrumentalist stopped asking *for what* a church body
should be an instrument. In the present instance, they were
not instruments at all for contributing to solutions after the
question, Is Christ divided? The Christians among them
pretty much repudiated all other Christians. Even less
could one build a republic out of them, taken together, or
any one of them, should one prevail.

Scholars who universalize and say that all past religion
has been persecutory make another law of history out of
something they observe in the West. Thus the Decree of
Asoka (264-228 B.C.) is a Buddhist judgment: "It is
forbidden to deny other sects; the true believer gives honor
to whatever in them is worthy of honor." Hinduism
survived through many cultural epochs while being
perplexingly absorptive and adaptive—and still full of

conviction. Jews, who have the book of Joshua and ancient exclusivism in their lore, have long since repudiated efforts to inflict the price of uncivility on others. Christians have not been consistently fanatic or persecutory. For centuries some leaders have tried to find ways for them to blend conviction with civility, to help them come to terms with strangers. The jihad may be an article of Islamic faith, but in some eras Jews were safer on Muslim soil than on Christian, and Christians of various sorts were better protected from one another under Islam than under their own competing regimes.

While the word *tolerance* is tainted and *civility* is under part of a cloud, it is not likely that they will disappear from the vocabulary. In the public sphere I find good reason to help reinstate the civil concept. But it has to be reinvested now with obscured meanings. Years ago in his *Creative Fidelity* Gabriel Marcel developed an inelegant but appropriate concept that he called "counter-intolerance." A person is always tolerant of or toward something. Like intolerance, tolerance must have an object. They are, neither one of them, merely moods. Tolerance becomes profound only when it comes from someone so convinced of something that intolerance was first a temptation. Counterintolerance is an outlook grounded in principle. I warrant it by the depth of my own conviction, says Marcel. To the extent that I hold to my view, I envisage another individual or group doing the same. I put myself in the other's place. "My awareness of my own conviction is somehow my guarantee of the worth" of the other's. Such an approach does not mean that I dare not re-present my conviction and invite others to my community. People who value commitments deeply do not have to feel superior or be aggressive if they wish to spread them, or hope that others will join them. But never can I use force or deception, or make proselytism the focus of my relation to others. If I do, says Marcel, I will seem "a servant of a God of prey whose goal it is to annex and enslave," and that is a loathsome image of God.

An image of God is at stake in all this. Since I first read Marcel it has been impossible for me to be content with nostalgia for an age of true belief in the form of persecution and intolerance. Never again after this insight would I be able to support approaches to mission that made God into a predator, even if I shrouded this concept in the language of love. Otherwise God's existence could depend too much upon my ability to pounce on others. God would have an identity that depended upon the skill and energy with which I built thick and high walls around my tribe and values. Faith would turn into mere nervousness. This whole resolve, not a turn from one way of life to another but from one way of receiving God to another, is at the center of my journey in faith. I had only to translate counterintolerance into an idea already at home in the vocabulary: responsiveness.

Rosenstock-Huessy wrote that we exist by a mighty entreaty. We listen to all kinds of human imperatives. When we relate to others, though we stammer and stutter, we "justify our existence by responding to this call." The God of promise invites response, and we freely come back with a counterpledge. Naturally, among humans we still expect weapons behind outstretched arms. Violence remains the dirty secret of history. Trust comes expensively. But the risk of responsiveness no longer signals that I must hold my convictions lightly. To do so would be to live with God not as a predator but as the ground of ultimate insecurity. In Quaker terms, responsiveness means civility "by convincement," a word that carries overtones of conversion—it is not natural to me—and conviction—it grows strong through reinforcings.

To some philosophers this idea of being responsive, civil

by convincement, has to be grounded in the idea of a pluralistic universe. William James, an embodiment of responsiveness, was a prophet of such a pluralism, yet even he saw a "unity-in-multiplicity." But monists and monotheists, for whom the universe is finally one—as when in Jesus Christ "all things hold together"—can make creative use of the pluralism that will face them until the end of history. As a Jesuit, a Thomist, and a Catholic, John Courtney Murray was a convinced monist, in reference to "beyond history." In a decisive passage he was sure, he said, that religious pluralism was "against the will of God," in the sense of the original intention or the final fulfillment of history. But, he added, pluralism *is* the human condition. It is written into the script of history. It will not marvelously cease to trouble the human city. Less sure than he about knowing the will of God, I more than agree about the human condition. It will not cease marvelously to trouble the human city. In this phrase I have relocated one word.

In the House of Muumbi or "the true visible church on earth" it is not necessary to ask how or whether God is active in other ways beyond the tribe. The tribal deity was the spirit or god of our hill, our lake, our tree, our tents, our tower, our system, our jurisdiction. Landscapes beyond one's own were unknown or, at best, so dim that they demanded no explanation or encounter. Once one overcomes pluralistic ignorance, three choices remain. A person can return to the tribe and reinforce it as if nothing of value exists beyond it. The conservative turns fundamentalist. Second, one can let awareness of other truths be overwhelming and let mere relativism take over. The moderate turns faithless. But one can also conceive of God in such a way that many forms of divine activity are mediated beyond the ways a particular tribe witnesses to them or grasps them.

Schubert Ogden will not recognize one of his insights in

the use I will here make of it, since I must translate into the
temporal language of the historian what he asserts in less
mythic theological terms: for the Christian, the God who is
revealed in Jesus Christ does not have something other in
mind to say or do than what was originally intended in the
whole creation. In intention, nature converges with what
grace now must supply. The Fall made this grace and New
Creation necessary. Some have called this Fall a *felix culpa,* a
fortunate guilt, because it necessitated the gift of Jesus
Christ and thus brought with it immeasurable joy in the new
realm that made grace urgent. (Some days I could tolerate a
paradise before or apart from the mixed benefits of the
Fall.) This point does not solve all the missionary problems
or address all the questions about "saving" faith. Such
questions have priority but no monopoly in the heart of the
sinsick, the missioner, and the theologian. But on a day
when Christian humanists are busy with civil questions they
have to move on to a second issue.

This issue relies on a distinction between saving faith
and ordering faith. Trouble results when people confuse
them. Thus some groups in America propose that the
human city would be untroubled if only the saved, the
born again, ran the government. Against them comes a
crass word of Luther, more crudely translated: better be
ruled by a smart Turk than a dumb Christian. God works
also through smart Turks. Whatever saving faith is, it is
not at the base of the state. Civil order, citizenship, and
good morals do not depend on it. The Christian under
grace and the humane person in nature are capable of
achieving similar human ends, though from partly
different motives. The Christian, fortunately, has no
exclusive claim on social justice or truth.

In one of the spheres of life the good news of God's saving
activity in Jesus Christ is for the Christian the *dynamis* or

power of God "unto salvation." In that sphere, the mandates of God do not rescue people. They do nothing but drive one to the zone where grace is a gift. On the other hand, the law of God is also a *dynamis,* a power of god, but it is for the care of the neighbor. The ordering of society prospers.

Christian history has numerous underdeveloped resources for this vision. In the heritage of Augustine and the Reformation is the concept of a *justitia civilis,* a civil righteousness that does not save but fosters good ordering and justice. This supplements a vision of "common grace" in which God is generally and naturally active in a world that is not divinely abandoned because of the Fall or the demonic. To limit the civil activity of God to one's own tribe and house is to reduce and cramp divine activity. When this occurs, as one book title had it, *Your God Is Too Small.*

Christians find natural partners with reflective Jews on subjects like these. One formula about a small but elect people puts it this way: the God of Israel does not depict all the world becoming Jewish so that the divine can be active in it. But God does regard Judaism as being necessary for what is to be worked out in the world. This understanding provides a basis of contact between peoples of two faiths or two types of faith in a way that replaces the old pounce-and-prey approach. It assures measures of responsiveness between houses whose common history has frequently been bloodied by Christian aggressiveness.

The topic of Judaism is appropriate here because of the part Jews play in the academy and other centers of civil discourse and effort. But a deeper reason lies in the roots of Judaism because of a common biblical legacy. What are some scriptural witnesses to this picture of God? The first thing most people know about the Hebrew Scriptures is that their jealous Lord deals with an elect and exclusive people. But Israel, "a light to the nations" and a people of conviction, had a mission. Both the prophets Isaiah and Micah foresaw the day when the nations would come and adore Yahweh in the sanctuary at Zion. All peoples would find their center there. Second Isaiah uses irony to show how futile it was to worship the silent gods of the pagans. "All were born in Zion" is the shout recorded in Psalm 87:5. When Christians read their present ordering of the Old Testament they come to the universal note at its end, in Malachi 1:11: "For from the rising of the sun to its setting my name is great among the nations, and in every place incense is offered in my name, and a pure offering; for my name is great among the nations, says the Lord of hosts."

While scholars debate the full meaning of that text, they agree that it leaves no one content with tribal exclusivism. And if it is not disruptive of the huddle, the prophecy of Amos is. Of course, Israel has a special relationship to the Lord: "You only have I known of all the families of the earth" (Amos 3:2a). And then, just when the walls of the solemn assembly confine and the ceiling is low, we hear, "therefore I will punish you for all your iniquities" (Amos 3:2b). A strand of Jewish humor ever since has complained about the inconvenience of being elected.

Throughout Amos, divine influence keeps stretching toward the universal, until near the end comes an attack on exclusivism:

"Are you not like the Ethiopians to me,
    O people of Israel?" says the Lord.
"Did I not bring up Israel from the land of Egypt,
    and the Philistines from Caphtor and the Syrians from Kir?"
                                                    (Amos 9:7)

Amos (6:2) shatters the foundations of any House of Muumbi, which claims a biblical basis for unresponsiveness. Of those who are at ease in Zion, he asks, "Are they better than these [other] kingdoms? Or is their territory greater than your territory . . .?"

Another disturber of the peace to the American majority that claims the biblical tradition is Isaiah 44–45. There Cyrus the Persian, who is to deliver exiled Israel, is called "my shepherd" by the Lord who says Cyrus "shall fulfill all my purpose" in building Jerusalem. In the divine scheme, a pagan thus inherits the role of David of Israel. The "my" implies an intimacy that throws a new light on secular or pluralist history. The prophet even calls Cyrus the *mashiah*, the anointed or messiah or Christos—words that acquire a sacred ring in the corridors of later history. The God of Israel, not the gods of the conqueror, anointed him. His "right hand I have grasped, to subdue nations before him. . . . to open doors before him that gates may not be closed" (Isa. 45:1). Cyrus may not even know of the God of Israel. No matter.

I have been unable to confirm a story that concerns Harry S Truman, told about an occasion when Jewish Theological Seminary wanted to honor the President for his contribution to the restoration of Israel in 1948. When Truman heard the citation, he placed himself among the outsiders of Second Isaiah and shrugged off his own contribution. But then with a biblical sense that many of the born again forget, this Sunday school alumnus went on, "I am Cyrus, I am Cyrus."

The New Testament deals more with saving than ordering, but Paul wagers that the world will be better off with civil order than not. "The powers that be are ordained of God." And there is Cornelius, a true ethnic of "the Italian Cohort" at Caesarea. This military person was "a devout man who feared God with all his household, gave alms liberally to the people, and prayed constantly to God." The voice of God came to him and acknowledged these prayers and alms. New-Christian Peter had not yet converted this man who was neither a Jew though he was friendly to Jews, nor a reborn Christian. In short, he was not a finished product. But he was some sort of "God-fearer," and he was credited with a kind of virtue apart from baptism.

Peter was a slow learner, but at last he was moved to say (Acts 10:34-35): "Truly I perceive that God shows no partiality, but in every nation any one who fears him and does what is right is acceptable to him." Standing somewhere between civic virtue and the orbit of the saved, Cornelius unsettles the exclusivists and judges the unresponsive. His before-and-after character illustrates a theme Mary McCarthy somewhere proposed: that religion makes good people good and bad people bad.

These brushes with theology are rather heady for someone who is called only to be *nur ein gewöhnlicher Historiker;* the university pays me to be "only a conventional historian." Any extension of thought about that role in realms where we have to "go up higher" is pure moonlighting. But at a pluralistic university, where the stories a historian tells reach far beyond the sanctuaries of the chosen people, this biblical outlook is a spur. On the few days when research looks sterile and inquiry seems beside the point, Amos and Cyrus and Cornelius are pick-me-ups.

While as a religious genius Martin Luther said something on opposite sides of most issues, but always with passion, I have torn out one page and made it a charter. The passage depicts a world in which I have to be more than tolerant, more than civil: responsive. "For because histories describe nothing other than God's work—that is grace and wrath—which we must so worthily believe as if they stood in the Bible, they should certainly be written with the greatest diligence, faithfulness, and truth."

And let it go at that? Or is one called to move from responsive attitudes to responsible action? The historian as historian need only tell stories, but the human being is sometimes called to participate in them. That, too, is part of the journey of faith.

5

Responsibility:
Politics and Beyond

"You don't splatter semen on the walls when you talk. You lecture just like a pro*fess*or." That is how I remember a shouted tribute to the eros of the late Paul Goodman and an attack on the limits of my own radicalism. The interrupter of my speech was a stormy devotee of Goodman who was correct in both her shouts. She was not alone in offering high-pitched criticism on a steamy summer evening in 1965, but I remember her best because she was my first contact with the new left critics who came to scorn intellectual moderation. Her kind supplemented the old right critics who thought all along that we should stick to our books and leave the world as it was. Between the two, ten years of the journey often seemed precarious. They provided a different context for decision about responsible action than many of us have known before or since. But they occasioned thought about its meaning that stays with us still.

To get back to the activist critic: her scene was Philosophy Hall at Columbia University. Its windows opened on two bus lines, and the sounds of New York traffic made lecturing difficult. Yet most of the noise that night came from within, in protest against a professor who was condemned for not being the lively anarchist Paul Goodman and for having been willing to comment, not wholly critically, on the then-dying Great Society.

In the midst of the disruptions I plunged ahead with analysis, until suddenly a hulking man, shrouded in his dark overcoat, charged the podium while recklessly swinging his umbrella. His great black beard made him look like a picture of an early Bolshevik, but his message differed from theirs. He started shouting at the crowd and the Great Society analyst, "Twenty-six million Americans can't be wrong! Twenty-six million Americans can't be wrong!" His was the now-forgotten battle cry of the defeated supporters of presidential candidate Barry Goldwater after 1964. His shout served as a momentary reminder to the Goodmanites that their victim that evening, while certainly beneath contempt, was still second-worst in the hierarchy of contemptibles. Enough people thereupon rallied to elicit sympathy and permit my completion of the lecture. At that, I still fared as well as old peacemonger, A. J. Muste, whom no Goldwaterite rescued, or the *Daseins*-analyst who followed in the same series. That doctor ended his speech abruptly after throwing his notes at the unsettlers with a "You kids shut up! You kids shut up!"

For several years they refused to shut up, and the evening at Columbia was followed by more tense successors on many campuses before the student generation lapsed back into apathy—while the professors kept on talking. Before the quiet came, they would post banners, like the one that graced our Divinity School entrance during the moratorium on academic work imposed after the bombing in Cambodia and the murders at Kent State, "What did you do in the war, Daddy? I studied." Revolutionary activism was to be the only licit vocation. Instead I studied revolutionary activism in light of a prior commitment toward responsible politics as the way for now, in our culture.

The Columbia scene followed by only two years my transit from parish to podium. Pastoral ministers in a voluntary society may be prophets, but they have to know they are politicians. Between pulpit and pew there is a not–always–subtle tugging, as one side or another cajoles or tantalizes the other into some sort of action— or embodies it, and then lets the other deal with it conceptually. To move too far or too fast means a break in the congregational relation and a possible dispersal of the group. Not to move at all means to settle for the world as it is, which is simply incongruent with all biblical mandates to such groups. Because of this immediate responsiveness by congregations, ministers hold political power that most professors and editors lack. In the sixties, one could take part in certain kinds of controversial activities in the field of racial justice or peace and gain status for doing so in the university or in journalism. That is hardly a way to be prophetic. Meanwhile, ministers had to go back and explain why they followed a course of action or, in the face of advance guard laypeople, why they did not. Where the explanations were convincing, new kinds of action could follow. That was power.

Ministers and lay leaders find that ethical issues ordinarily come in undramatic forms: in decisions over zoning, racial integration, provision of mental health care, the condition of nursing homes, priorities in education, and the like. These did not ready a generation of Christians to deal with the gross divisions in American life over race and war. For the foreseeable ethical issues in the years ahead, many of which have to do with complexities in medicine or the uses of energy and the environment, they may have been a better schooling. Ready or not, at a decisive turn in the road the call came to be counted on race and war. I will rehearse only enough of the story to set the framework for an issue: what the way of response does to an appraisal of various elements in a decision.

For ten years I devoted many energies in writings, speeches, and action to the epochal ethical issue of race relations and civil rights in America. I was always aware of my limits, derived as they were from problems of understanding location, vocation, and cowardice. Toward the midsixties, blacks were in the process of determining the direction of their movement. I could see a diminishing role for white leadership even in the black or integrated congregations I had served in student days a decade before. And when housing came to be the central issue, we Martys were compromised because of where we lived. To our northwest was an almost all-black community, to the west a black enclave inside a white suburb, toward the south, industry, and east of us some pure white "ethnic" communities backed up against the most devastated black ghettos in Chicago.

We chose our town because it was equidistant to my three bases, downtown, the university community, and the airport—and because it charms the heart of historians. The village is an antique landmark, America's oldest planned suburb (by the great Frederick Law Olmsted), and not an address that gives credibility to advocates of justice in housing patterns—for the simple reason that the public is most stirred when its agitators have something themselves to risk. A metropolitan daily religion editor did me the favor of pointing this out very early in the game. She was rather salty about how her colleagues and readers did not take seriously the preachments on community change by any of the "S.O.Bs from the National Council of Churches on down," because they lived "safely away from the scene of change, in New Jersey or Westchester County or in highrises with doormen and lots of security."

Schooling was another consideration in our choice of a middle-class community in a metropolis where that meant little integration. It had become part of our vocation, indeed, my wife's field of specialty, to elaborate the idea of "the extended family." This meant extending our own in ever-changing ways. For twenty years it has involved the inclusion in our family of two children from a Mexican-American family, occasional young people from the ghetto in summer, year-round custodianship of two young boys from Uganda, foreign students, and an occasional stray. University colleagues usually sent their children to private or laboratory schools which, though delightfully integrated racially, were socially and intellectually stratified and less representative of the city at large than our own U.N.-style household. The alternative in the university locale would have been to send children to the then-substandard public schools or dividing the house between "our" children in private schools and our passing-through children in public schools. That would obviously have been intolerable.

While our multiethnic family was not designed to prove anything racially or to disturb the neighbors—many of whom identified warmly with our concept of extended family life—it did upset some. Such occasions kept the urgency of change in racial attitudes before us. Once we served coffee through an originally calm evening of conversation in our living room. A gentleman had dropped by to explain that his aged mother did not like it that one of our boys had stepped on her lawn. We explained that through the years we assumed such a transgression must have ocurred before; it happened whenever a child hit a home run. He smiled, but his lips grew tense, "This was different. It mattered *which* boy stepped there." He told us that when his mother was upset he was upset and when he was upset he did not earn money. Somehow everything seemed very rational when he changed the tone slightly, tensed the lip line more, and leaned forward, "And if it happens again, I'll kill you."

Neither he nor my wife ever doubted that he meant it. And then came torrents of accusation. He was a Presbyterian and I was a supporter (however fainthearted) of "the communist Rev. John Fry" who worked with black gangs. Our visitor left. No ball or boys' foot ever fell on that lawn again. John Fry moved away. The gun, I presume, is no longer in our visitor's car. His mother has died, and we still pour tea and coffee for guests.

My mind floods with memories: of the times when my wife and sons were between forces during and on the ride home from church school in the black community at the heart of the Lawndale and West Garfield Park rioting. Of the heavy breathing treatment from a realtor who harassed us with 9:30 and 2:30 daily phone calls after a really rather docile speech I had made. Of how the telephone company found a way to help us trace the call and find who our tormentor was, only to read a few days later that the Lord gathered him to his heavenly rest. Of the time I outdrew previous baccalaureate speakers when we were going to surprise our foster daughter by appearing at her high school graduation. It happened that the members of a nearby same-faith church, who did not like it that I was "an associate of America-hating Martin Luther King, Jr.," started a campaign on a call-in radio show to have the invitation recalled and me, the immoralist, removed from the program.

I had years before gained an awareness of my ineffectuality in the field of race relations within the Christian church. In thirty years of preaching there has been only one chance to verify empirically the effect of my thundering.

While a graduate student serving southside black parishes, I was suddenly reassigned to a German-speaking church in a changing community. Its members, I was told, had just voted to abandon the building and its mission, to sell it to a not-yet-existent black parish. I agreed to preach there if they would let me read German sermons. Extempore Germanizing was out of the question. For six weeks they heard my memorized sermons by Eduard Thurneysen, with only the phrase *unser Zwingli sagt,* "Our (Reformed pioneer) Zwingli says," changed to *unser Luther sagt.*

I was also free to preach on the prophets and racial justice in their better-attended English services. It would be my goal to show how they could usher in a new day in the kingdom of God if they would reconsider their vote to leave, with a view then to leaving behind a remnant for gradual transition to the inevitable black parish that would follow the move. The members agreed so I preached and they voted. Before the sermons, I believe, the score was something like 83–2 against staying; after them a straw vote went 85–3. On the way home thereafter an obliging senior member who was my chauffeur tried to console me. "You know, pastor, you got it all wrong about who's holding this church together. You think it's the Germans. You're wrong. We're Austrian!" I am not sure the Austrians were ready for integration with the Germans, to say nothing of the new blacks. It was, by the way, these people who later were the only ones ever to call me to be their pastor.

Being a historian is admittedly one of the less adequate vocations to prepare one for racial forms of social action. Unless they approach their subject with a declared ideology like Marxism, historians will be suspicious of grand systems. They are trained to probe all human motivations and to carry low expectations about the possibility of human change. Historians ordinarily do not expect to see people soar. They are content to find anyone being nudged at all for an inconveniencing cause—and then they spend the rest of the day checking out what could possibily have moved the movers. Most of them have little use for the Manichaeism or utopianism of the revolutionary who would destroy the old order and foresee the new phoenix emerge from the ashes. Behind every social pronouncement they issue a thousand qualifications. Behind every demonstration there are a score of ways for them to charter foot-dragging.

All this means that historians who feel called to intervene in history on modest personal scales will usually choose political action as their instrument. I love party politics and find myself responding to the sight and sound of conventions, caucuses, precinct organization, banners and buttons, platforms and speeches, ballot boxes and arguments. While my profession keeps me from a full engagement, I have been pleased to see a couple of sons show signs of devoting their life to the political calling. They and I know that it is not a world for prophetic purists, but rather for those who seek human good while making use of partisan interests. We are meliorists at heart. That means, wherever we are on the political spectrum, to cherish the rule of law and to seek redress of grievances within it. Most responsibility follows the lines of this circumscribed zone of politics. But what do we do when existing law contradicts the intentions of the republic, limits the expression of Christian and other human freedoms, or violates conscience and a higher law—and does so not accidentally and momentarily but in a sustained and profound way?

One must also act responsibly in such extraordinary times. At a decisive moment in American history, almost miraculously, a group of historians took part in the Selma to Montgomery march. They were never able to regather forces when the opposition became more fierce, as it did in northern cities. I did not go with the historians but with a gathering of leaders who, as Christians, do not live by an ideology but by an impulse that asks them at times to forget their footnotes and foot-dragging.

The call from Martin Luther King, Jr., to help fill a plane of Chicagoans to start the Selma march was too compelling to deny. Inside my London Fog coat pockets my wife jammed some Metrecal Wafers—"They expand inside the stomach; who knows when you'll get to eat again?" In the other pocket I put a flask of Scotch "for medicinal purposes." Next day on the Pettis Bridge as we faced the lawmen I could envision the possible onset of diarrhea. Instead of keeping my mind only on the King-led prayer—of such irrational confusions pseudo-activists are made—I pictured a headline that would delight racist foes: "Theologian Arrested for Exposure. Liquor Found on His Person." By evening, the Reverend Jim Reeves was dead and we were escaping to Atlanta.

A *Time* correspondent who hitchhiked back with five of us Divinity School faculty members to Atlanta heard us evaluate our acts that day. We had begun to march not against an Alabama statute but a Federal Court injunction. Was that being responsible? We were all biblical scholars or historians. One was a Tory Anglican who was not yet sure that the British king was off the scene in America. Two were Lutherans who were obsessed with the issues of whether they had violated Romans 13, an injunction against disobedience to authority. Our rider, after hearing all our reservations and rationales, remarked wryly that he was not sure we *had* marched. Yet we had responded. Whatever posterity thinks of the event—and fifteen years later, alas, many were embarrassed about the idealism it revealed—it did help bring about change at the point where research and theorizing gave out.

No tales of heroism followed. When King later marched five miles from my home, I must not have been ready for what my student, a nun, showed me. On her arm was a bruise "caused by a Catholic brick." We do come to terms easily with the face of evil close to home. One day a British journalist and I strolled from lunch on Michigan Avenue. "What would happen," he asked casually, "if a black family tried to move into _____?" He named an all-white ethnic enclave proverbial for its resistance to the black ghetto across the boundary. I gave him my answer. When he returned to England, the Britisher wrote in his column that he had asked the same question of a dozen Chicagoans. Not one, he wrote, missed a beat, lost a step, or took a second for thought or offered a second thought. Not one seemed to be shocked or aware of shocking as each answered, in effect, "The house would be bombed and the family run out or killed."

Now, you may think I tell that story to show how evil one town was. Instead I will verge on sentimentalizing its citizens at the risk of contributing to moral immobility. Nothing I could say would excuse such a potentially murderous consequence. I would play the barbarian even to let the possibility of a rationale for it to flit across the mind. But: it happens that I know those citizens well. In communities like theirs I have preached, dined, served on hospital boards, and both known and observed friendships.

"Ethnics" live there, many of them survivors of the Nazi-Stalinist vise that squeezed middle Europe. They proved their heroism in wartime. They demonstrated their generosity to their kind and others ever since. They are no special breed of monster. Many of them are especially warm lovers of their families and clans. Most are frugal investors who have paid for their home but own little else. They want to stay put, tired as they are of having been displaced persons. They could not cope while staying, enjoy the new company, or pack off so easily "when the neighborhood changes," as could we in academic and middle-class communities. In Chicago many communities upgrade, so far as citizen education and income are concerned, when blacks move in, but most whites do not act that way. In the view of a white community a relentless logic follows upon its own premises. Here is how a member of such a neighborhood, aware of current real estate policies and practices, would state the case: the first black (or, translate Hispanic) on a block means, months later, a changed block. Thus, a black block means three years later, a black town. Blacks who want to move to new communities in a metropolis like Chicago know they are as much a victim of these policies as are whites. Most people we know have to be free to act free. There have to be circumstances on which they can rely for some security if they are to make moves that invite other insecurities. Little in housing practices help them.

The prophet of God, I hear some say, would thunder in tones of Amos against people who make so much of their equity and investments that they become an idol while others suffer. But I questioned whether the activist anarchist in Philosophy Hall had the credentials to be a prophet at all. One of the reasons the public conscience was so seldom stirred by abrupt denunciations was that the denouncers had not yet exemplified a way of life superior to the one they would replace. The effective leaders like King himself *had* done so. That is why he was successful and why he had to be killed.

Too often I saw creative potential in the very people who were written off by the more revolutionary and less empathic activists. When racial change first came, we who lived in farther-out suburbs or urban strongholds derided the "old ethnics" who moved away. When the time came to become acquainted with and serve the churches in racially changing communities, it was often to see that only the aged white women had stayed behind. Some did so out of nostalgia for neighborhoods, others for lack of funds, a few out of conviction. Who needs to know which was which? The point is that they came to know and live with new people who were so utterly foreign to their experience. Sometimes during the riots and burnings they teamed up with senior blacks who were also trapped amid the bombings and fires, to appeal to the farther-outs to put them up together through the worst. I came away from the decade with few ideas as to how to change the community except not to settle for benign neglect, but with the resolve not to overlook such people or merely to put them down.

When it came time to take a stand about the prosecution of the war in Vietnam, many of us had to act despite some ignorance about details of foreign policy and Southeast Asian military affairs. How could one speak out responsibly? Yet we tried. In retrospect it would seem that our eventual hundred million, half-informed and full of instinct alone as we often were, had better perceptions than did the experts.

Yet the call to responsibility took much of the enjoyment out of dissent. At the worst possible and thus the most creative moment I read Jacques Ellul on *Violence*. Ellul is no passivist, but he can force activists to search their consciences. His book reminded us how easy it was to be for the fashionable poor. They were fashionable because we selected carefully among the victims those who could best advance our own cause. In this case, it meant bringing down a despised administration in Washington. Who spoke up for the unfashionable poor? How often did actual concern for the Vietnamese babies and the rural fields inspire dissent? Was that what lay behind the anarchy of the people in Philosophy Hall, or the tantrums of those who took over the Administration Building?

While no expert on foreign affairs, I had helped form groups like Clergy and Laity Concerned About Vietnam and signed all the right *New York Times* advertised declarations of conscience. Soon I was called to be a draft counselor. Would it be responsible to cooperate with the kind of student who on occasion would come to the office and say, "Professor, I've never been inside a church or synagogue. Can you give me enough theology to tide me over a meeting with my draft board?" No, I could not.

A generation of young men were emerging, however—people who by their previous way of life in tutoring, social service, and volunteer work showed that they were not merely interested in themselves or in trendy causes. To deny their request for counsel and representation in those days would have been simply irresponsible. All this sounds very safe and mild today, because for the decade to follow, the war was seen as having been so utterly immoral that *of course* all right-thinking moral people would have opposed it. But we were acting in the face of and against the law; selective conscientious objection was not and is not yet legal. Give us a few years, and a new generation of leftists-turned-rightists or doves-turned-hawks will engage in enough revisionism to make the war itself seem morally plausible. Then again our actions will appear to have been foolish and courageous.

This story I tell to take us back to the locale where the enemy of the activists purportedly gathered. One of my counselees had to appear before the draft board in a white-ethnic town where King had marched, where Christian bricks flew, and the hawks soared high. As we entered I was identified to the chairman of the draft board. "Are you *the* Martin E. Marty?" This question should have tripped my ego, but it only triggered my alarm. Is he identifying me with Martin Luther King, Jr., and racial threats to his front yard? Will I complicate life for my conscientious objector? Not at all. The man went on: "I wish my wife were here. She teaches in CDC classes at a Catholic parish. She reads you. Let's talk." However briefly, we talked: about how little he liked the war and his post, about how he was coming to see that there were more kinds of patriotism than one, about how we could better represent objectors in the future. We relished no victory that evening, but we did get a fair hearing. We had found ways to respond across separating boundaries and established the beginning of responsible action.

From these few observations along the journey it should come as no surprise to learn that I long ago handed in and found accepted a little card, "I hereby resign as boss of the universe." I have little taste and less prospect for finding prophets on every masthead or in every tenure contract. Centuries of history in Israel turned up only a few prophets who stung or saved anyone. Short of such moments, the way of criticism and politics has seemed more responsible, especially since it brings perspective to one's self and reckons with more interests of others.

Politics, it is often noted, is a minor art. Politics involves compromise. It cannot save souls or make sad hearts glad or bring in the kingdom of God. But it allows for a discernment of what makes other interest groups contend for what they do. Politics helps keep the losers alive, in the knowledge that on another day on another issue they might be creative partners. Politics helps separate what cannot be negotiated from what can. Sometimes it helps define those rare instances when people must abandon politics and engage in witness or gestures of direct action, no matter what the consequences, but for the sake of integrity.

These lines I write with full respect for the several people in the twentieth century—I count King and Day, Dietrich Bonhoeffer, Dom Helder Camara, and Steve Biko among them—who, though they were thoroughly political human beings, knew that their final responsibility to God was to act beyond normal principle and ordinary law. Without their passion we would be short of examples in a day when people perish for lack of vision. But to keep prophecy from lapsing into propheticism, witness from ego-tripping, siding with the oppressed to advancing one's own cause, it is important to reserve their kind of action for extreme cases. Paul Ricoeur has spoken of an "ethics of distress," which, if invoked, must be done in the interest of resuming other patterns of ethics soon after.

Those familiar with the proper names of Christian discourse will see here a preference for Niebuhrian Christian realism. It also relies on another Niebuhr's concept of the responsible self. Such a commitment is not satisfied to suppress the radical character of biblical mandates. The word of Jesus is uncompromising. But though what we hear of his word reaches us and will not let our conscience go, every act occurs in a world of bad choices and conflicting interests, many of them held by people who deserve responsiveness from those tempted to know too easily "what Jesus would do."

Ethical action is not part of the field of specialization of historians, a result of the way the modern academy chops up labor. Historians usually have a very modest role. They are not the messiah who can say, "It is written, but I say unto you." But historians do keep the record of the tradition, which has radical roots. They make these available to the person of conscience who appeals to it, "It is written, and I insist." No one can ever anticipate when that word of insistence will call one who was trained to be only a chronicler, who would like to be a mere bystander. When it does, along with it comes the test of responsible action—even in distress.

6
The Way Ahead

Within a generation the calendar will mark the end of the second millennium after Christ. The magic of the year 2000 began years ago to call forth scripts "Toward the Year 2000." The public tore them up before the ink was dry. What their writers called "surprise-free long-term multi-fold trends" lasted only a year or two. Fred Charles Ikle, one of the pre-scripters, noted that the scenario writers pictured the whole future in light of trends and issues of the year in which they wrote, "This marked tendency to select our topics for predictions from among our concerns of the most recent past should give us pause."

Alfred North Whitehead provided a longer perspective when he wrote that one could describe modern history under two categories: steam and democracy. One represented brute forces, the other ideology. In the early 1980s it is tempting to foresee the future only in terms of the present energy crisis and the limits to growth that come with it. Yet, despite Ikle and in the cosmic scope of Whitehead, it seems safe to say that for the rest of our lifetimes, at least as long as the world relies chiefly on nonrenewable sources of energy, their costs will grow and international relations will remain tense. Everything from the heating bills of religious institutions, weekend travel habits, and attendance at worship, to the politics of rationing and the question of shifting loyalties in the Middle East—or World War III—will somehow be connected with it. At all points this will have a bearing on ideology and spiritual concerns. But confident though I am *that* energy will be the urgent brute fact, I am not competent to discuss *how* it will be. Accepting the concept of that division of labor which comes with modernity, I choose to look down the road at some of the more or less ideological themes that will demand response in the believing communities.

Utopianism is not likely to remain as strong a theme as it was at midcentury in the West that was its home. The millennial theme is likely to be stronger. The magic of the year 2000 will trigger thought among numerologists about thousands of years. The record of the year 1000 c.e. and its context give no comfort to any who hope to avoid irresponsible apocalypticisms in the years ahead. The fact that earthly dreams have turned into nightmares and that "nothing works" will lead millions to misuse the biblical language about the urgency of the end-time. Like the author and ten million buyers of *The Late Great Planet Earth* they are likely to use this language for several purposes. They will act like *cognoscenti* about the future and thus build up their self-centered tribes. Then they will set out to rescue others of the elect to join them. It is likely that their approach will lead to a charter for hedonism, since they may as well enjoy waiting. And, most important, they will be free to be apathetic about changing a world that according to prophecy must get worse if Christ is to come.

Between the departing utopians and the arriving millenarians will be the company of realists who dare not let circumstance overwhelm them. If Christian, they will not underestimate the power of evil. In history, the demonic pervades existence. But they will refuse to believe it has the only word or the last word. In the midst of the certain threats and terrors, which are not the first that Christian history has seen, they will try to intervene on the course of history.

Christians and especially Christians of this sort will make up only a small cohort of humanity. While the world will keep its religious dimensions, in our culture secular elements are likely to dominate. While the passional side of human nature guarantees religious vitalities, the operative side finds religion to be in an ambiguous place. It serves to explain ever fewer aspects of existence to the whole population. The recent religious revivals have not to any great extent penetrated intellectual, literary, or academic cultures. The amount of energy Christian apologists have to devote to C. S. Lewis or T. S. Eliot only reinforces the point of the rarity of such figures. We are surprised when an author devotes a life to the Christian theme. We know that peers make no special place for them and find their symbols puzzling. The resurgently religious have also not reorganized approaches to knowledge in the university or priorities in the mass media.

Religion has had a free ride during these decades when society was off balance. While the world is not likely soon to get on balance, many in it are growing impatient with the false promises of extravagant solutions. While the sacred cow of science is now crippled, we can expect new warfares of science and religion to break out in the face of challenges posed by sociobiology, behaviorism, and the new astronomy. Secular intellectuals who ignored the claims of religion will react more vigorously as they see creationists and single-issue religious interests intrude on realms they consider their own. Tax exemption of such religious groups will face more challenges than before. Publics will expect more accountability from religious agencies since many of them have grown patently irresponsible. And as these agencies compete ever more viciously for the clientele dollar they will have to make claims and promises that will be ever harder to deliver. Expect more reaction. In sum: while the impulses behind religiosity will grow as people seek meaning, the momentum behind secularity will at the same time increase.

That's good. A clash of doctrines, said Whitehead, is an opportunity, not a disaster. Such a clash might lead to the reform of the Christian house. After a generation in which personal experience and mindless authority received such high premium, there are signs that the challenges are making some Christians think again. Believers have often been clearer-headed in the face of atheists than at the side of religious fellow-travelers.

Robert M. Hutchins once advised students, "Get ready for anything, because anything is what's going to happen. We don't know what it is, and it's very likely that whatever it is, it won't be what we think it is." My own getting ready follows three possible frameworks, allows anything to happen within them, and helps me anticipate some next steps on the journey.

The first of these frameworks foresees the reemergence of totalitarianisms of the sort that have dominated this century. Robert Heilbroner plausibly pictures that after economic collapse and reorganization Americans are not likely to go far without seizing on an ideology to justify their processes. They would then assent to a statist religion, since a complex society could not allow so much diversity as we now have, as it made its transit to a polity of control. This mild Maoism would not be called Marxism. A better prospect would be "Christian Democracy." The leaders of such a regime would appeal to symbols that already have roots in a pluralist society—and then allow for little religious freedom or dissent.

Obvious factors make this script credible. With the rise of terrorism in the nuclear age, citizens may feel or find that a society of total surveillance is necessary. As resources diminish and our present business civilization falls, they would not tolerate reallocations of goods without a creed that would impel conformity and sacrifices. Some who see the vitality of Christianity in a Poland look forward to such a polity as a test of faith and a spur to dissent. They overlook the price paid in Soviet Russia or the snuffing out of Christianity and other faiths in Maoist China.

The opposite extreme is pure individualism. Heilbroner talks about how citizens devote themselves now to merely "private morale." As in the civic, so in the religious realm. Ultramodern spirituality, whether conservative or liberal in theology, is invisible and private. Religion in a late capitalist and competitive order is purely consumerist. It then offers more substance than meaning. Advertisers of its benefits, whether in fundamentalist paperbacks, on entrepreneurial television, among fashionable therapies, or with do it yourself Eastern religious techniques, have to make ever more egregious claims in order to gain clienteles and customers.

Such religion gives no more than lip service to the organized church or religious institutions that are its real rivals. Gone are even the positive values of the tribe and the family. Tradition is packaged for instant consumption.

There are no deferred benefits, only instant gratifications. The cross of Jesus Christ remains a symbol for Christian versions of this new faith, but its original meanings are gone. No hint of Jesus's cry of abandonment by God is heard. This religion does not help devotees cope with the problem of evil. In place of calls for sacrifice there are promises of rewards in dollars and cosmetic appearance, physical perfection and athletic achievement, political success and new popularity. Such religion lacks social power. No two adherents agree on what to transmit to a new generation. There is no room for judgment or admonition of others in the company, for mutual consolation, for the republic or the *oikoumene*. It helps create the void that totalism would fill.

False alternatives, no matter how powerful, need not tyrannize. I have often seen an argument of Aristotle pointing to the framework for a third way. "The object which Socrates assumes as his premiss is . . . 'that the greatest possible unity of the whole *polis* is the supreme good.' Yet it is obvious that a *polis* which goes on and on, and becomes more and more of a unity, will eventually cease to be a *polis* at all. A *polis* by its nature is some sort of aggregation. If it becomes more of a unit, it will first become a household instead of a *polis,* and then an individual instead of a household. . . . . It follows that, even if we could, we ought not achieve this object: it could be the destruction of the *polis.*"

Bronislaw Malinowski has advised that "to scour the universe for possibilities of freedom other than those given by the organization of human groups for the carrying out of specific purposes, and the production of desirable results is an idle philosophic pastime." I am not the first to see this political model confirmed in the concept of the Dutch Calvinist Johannes Althusius. He foresaw a *communitas communitatum,* a community of communities or subcommunities. It stands between Leviathan and anarchic individualism.

This framework led to the ecumenical model that exists in the time between the complete unity that Jesus impelled into history and promises at its end. Here on earth the church is always in the process of becoming one, but now, under whatever polities, it is a "family of apostolic churches." Even these churches are themselves aggregates of smaller caucuses, congregations, interest groups, movements, and tribes. Each of them finds wholly private religion to be an enemy and a totalist world church a specter, though hardly an awesome one in this epoch. Today the *communitas communitatum* is torn apart by overly assertive tribalists who care little for the whole Christian *polis*.

This model is what has made it possible for us to celebrate tribes and decry tribalism. It led to a favoring of Benjamin Franklin's public religion over Rousseau's civil religion. It asks for people to probe their own traditions deeply in the hope that if these have an integrity they will lead inheritors to find people of other traditions to whom to respond. The deep people of this century, Gandhi and Buber, Pope John and King, Bonhoeffer and Mother Teresa, are all inexplicable apart from their own tribe, whose lore they have probed all their lives. And they come closest to being truly universal humans.

We began with recall of one person's symbol of tribe and tradition, a church whose walls were confining, whose ceilings were too low. But I do not profess to have exhausted the biblical lore that occasioned it, the confession or communion it engendered. The calling to be a historian taught more, not less, appreciation of its positive side. But that tradition also teaches us not to be content with a small tribal deity of our time, our tribe. The way of response calls for commitment to the God revealed in Jesus Christ—and openness to the surprising ways this God has acted beyond exclusive circles, according to the witness in earliest biblical times.

Historians are mappers more than pathfinders or road builders. They live *coram deo,* in the sight of God, and not *versus deum,* which would mean that through theory or piety they would gain the vision of God. And all along the journey of faith they tell stories. We live by their power. For this reason, I never feel a great breach between being a narrator, a historian, and being actively involved in the world.

Martin Buber gave new life to story when he said that it was itself an event and had the quality of a sacred action. It is more than a reflection, because the sacred essence to which it bears witness lives on in it. The wonder that is narrated becomes live and powerful once more. So Buber told a story about a rabbi whose grandfather had been a pupil of the great founder of Hasidism, Baal Shem Tov. This rabbi was once asked to tell a story. "A story ought to be told so that it is itself a help," and his story was as follows: "My grandfather was paralyzed. Once he was asked to tell a story about his teacher and he told how the holy Baal Shem Tov used to jump and dance when he was praying. My grandfather stood up while he was telling the story and the story carried him away so much that he had to jump and dance to show how the master had done it. From that moment, he was healed. This is how stories ought to be told."

I take my place in the company on a journey, hoping not to bore them with stories biblical, historical, and contemporary. All travelers on the Christian road have some sense of what Cervantes knew, that the road can be better than the inn. Meister Eckhart, a classic mystic put it well: "There is no stopping place in this life—no, nor was there ever one for any man, no matter how far along his way he'd gone. This above all, then, be ready at all times for the gifts of God and always for new ones." For the Christian there is, therefore, always and only a word calling for response. It comes from One who announced little about the point of arrival but said what his followers needed to know when He declared, "I am the way."